MARGARET BRANDMAN

Contemporary Piano Method
Junior Primer
for piano and electronic keyboard

Exclusive Distributors for Australia and New Zealand
Encore Music Distributors
227 Napier St. Fitzroy Vic 3065 Australia
Phone: +61 3 9415 6677
Facsimile: +61 3 9415 6655
Email: sales@encoremusic.com.au

This book © Copyright 2020 by Margaret Brandman trading as Jazzem Music
46 Gerrale St. Cronulla NSW 2230 Australia
ISBN 978-0-949683-00-7
Order No. MMP 8077
Illustrations by Don Ezard
Editing & design by Glen Hannah
International Copyright Secured (APRA/AMCOS) All Rights Reserved

Unauthorised reproduction of any part of this publication by any means including photocopying is an infringement of copyright.

Contents

3	Introduction		36	Playing Steps and Sames – *Song of Two Hills*
6	SECTION ONE – The Basics – Seating Position			*Marching On The Spot Song*
7	Hand Position		37	A Picture Song to Play – *Lightly Row*
8	Keyboard Geography		38	Songs to Play – *Song of Hills and Plains*
9	Feeling for the Signpost Notes			*Rain is Falling Down*
10	Signpost Notes		39	Musical Shapes & Patterns – *Nifty Shape-Shifter*
11	Notes On The Staff			*A Catchy Tune*
12	A Musical Map – High & Low Sounds		40	SECTION THREE – Reading & Playing Skips
13	Exploring Low, Middle & High Sounds		41	Skipping Easy – Up & Down
14	Getting to Know the Music Ladder & Intervals		42	More Skips To Play
15	Feeling Intervals			*Skipping Easy Round The Town, Skipping Easy Up & Down*
16	Activity Page – Writing Intervals			*Fun With Skips*
17	A Picture Song to Play		43	More Musical Shapes & Patterns
	Ode To Joy			*Another Nifty Shape-Shifter*
18	Rhythm in Music			*A Pretty Song of Steps & Sames*
19	Rhythm Quiz		44	Longer Pieces of Music – *Mary Had A Little Lamb*
20	Colour & Clap – Colour Chart		45	Night-time Songs – *Au Clair De La Lune*
21	Activity Page – Colour & Clap			*Suogan*
22	The Great Staff and Middle C		46	A Sea Shanty – *Long Legged Sailor*
23	Improvising		47	Playing in Waltz Time - …….*waltz?*
24	SECTION TWO – Reading & Playing Steps & Sames		48	A Spooky Tune – *Swinging Ghost Song*
25	Follow The Flow		49	Playing In March Time – *Goblin March*
26	Write and Play Steps – The See-Saw Song		50	A Piece To Perform – *Sunday Song*
27	*Wiggling Steps*		51	SECTION FOUR – Two New Intervals – Skip-plus-One
28	Signpost C's		52	The Jump
29	Follow The Flow from High & Low C		53	A Picture Song To Play
30	Musical Shapes & Patterns: Similar Motion		54	Activity Page – Compare these Intervals
	Stepping Easy – *Up and Down*		55	Playing Jumps – *Cherokee Jumping Song*
31	Stepping Easy – *Down and Up*		56	Activity Page – Writing – Keyboard Name Games
32	Writing Activity – Keyboard Name Games		57	Playing Skip-plus-Ones – *Chop Suey Song*
33	A Picture Song To Play		58	Tunes Using All Five Intervals – *What's The Matterhorn?*
34	Musical Shapes & Patterns: Contrary Motion		59	*Traffic Lights*
	Stepping Easy – *Out & In*		60	*Johnny Works With One Hammer*
35	Stepping Easy – *In & Out*		61	Award Certificate

Introduction

The Contemporary Piano Method is designed to equip the student with the necessary skills to play both Classical and Modern (Popular and Jazz) music, with ease and understanding, and covers skills required for both classical and contemporary examination syllabi. The piano method is the central core of an integrated course, which provides materials for ear-training, (audio and workbooks) theory, improvisation and repertoire pieces in all styles. The Junior Primer is designed as a gradual lead in to the method for the 5 to 11 age group. Students will be able to continue directly in to Book 1A once they have completed the primer.

The methodology incorporates various learning styles or modalities, including:

- ★ aural training
- ★ spatial reasoning - visual, aural and tactile
- ★ the gestalt approach
- ★ visualisation and the use of pictorial representations of intervals
- ★ knowledge of keyboard geography
- ★ shape and pattern reading
- ★ harmonic analysis
- ★ improvisation
- ★ colour - to impart the meaning of the duration of notes via spatial diagrams and through the act of colouring in.
- ★ gross motor actions to understand direction concepts and to establish a body feel for timing through clapping.
- ★ fine motor actions to understand direction concepts and for musical technique

A unique feature of the method is the accompanying *Contemporary Piano Method* DVD in which many of the special teaching techniques are demonstrated. This DVD is useful for students and teachers alike.

Creativity Corner - Improvisation and creative work

The first section of this book encourages students to experiment with sounds to explore the piano and at the same time develop the technique required to play the more formal reading passages later in the book. Other opportunities for improvisation occur throughout the book.

Steps and Skips - The simplified interval approach

The series introduces a versatile and flexible way to read music, through a simplified interval approach, which combines the aural, tactile, vocal and visual aspects of music into one neat package. Even more effective than the usual numerical system for interval sizes, use of the easy interval language shown in this book, can help the swift transference of the picture of the distance between two notes (interval) to the feeling in the hand and the aural impression of the sound. This means that students no longer have to look down at the keyboard to search for each note and consequently rely more on other faculties such as ear and touch, leaving the eyes free to follow the music. The added benefit of this easy language is that the confusion between numbers for intervals, numbers for counting, and finger numbers is eliminated.

Anchor Points

In this book the notes C and F are used as signpost notes. As the C's are easy to locate on the keyboard layout, both visually and by touch, this also allows the interval reading system to be extended in the further books in this series, to reading above and below the staff and into C Clef.

Follow the flow...

The system encourages students to see music as a flowing chart while moving around the keys by means of spatial reasoning, tactile response and a consistent use of aural skills for pre-hearing and correction. As soon as two notes are played in succession, the ear begins to recognise the motif or essential idea of a song, and can build on that perception. In this book, the sizes of the intervals are represented pictorially by characters on staircases to impart the idea of how many keys are stepped along, or skipped over.

The whole view (Gestalt) - Music Speed reading by shapes and patterns

Reading by following the flow of the intervals and the contour of the musical line, enhances shape and pattern reading, (for example chords and scalic passages) as an aid to sight reading and speed learning of pieces. Shape and pattern reading also provides the foundation for the understanding of keys, chords and the harmonic structure of a piece.

Even more flexibility and versatility

Once students understand the easy concepts and can transfer the message to their fingers, they are able to:
- a) play with both hands together more readily as the reading for both parts uses similar information, rather than two sets of note names
- b) play on the staff lines or on leger lines with equal ease
- c) transpose to various areas of the keyboard. If white note patterns are shifted they can produce interesting 'modal' sounds. (See for instance pages 41 and 42 of this book)
- d) transpose to all keys - provided that the scale patterns on the keyboard are learnt as a pre-requisite as is done on Book One of the series.
- e) sing the intervals as they play using the language of Step, Skip etc. This will enable them to learn to sight-sing and at the same time quickly develop aural perception.

Easy ways to conceptualise rhythm and rhythm notation

The use of diagrams to be coloured in and then clapped, helps children quickly associate a concrete meaning to the new language of music rhythm notation and establish a body feel for timing. The use of colour, spatial concepts and the tactile information transferred by the act of colouring, brings into play many accelerated learning concepts.

Direction concepts

Using the gestalt view of intervals, students are more readily able to see a larger section of music in one glance so that the combined direction of the notes for both hands becomes more obvious. This helps greatly in the early stages of learning in the actual process of coordinating the hands and relaying the message to the fingers.

Each piece should be prepared by:

      a) clapping through the note values   *and*   **b)** talking or singing the intervals, direction and counting

★ To develop the pitches for vocal and ear-training, students should be encouraged to sing the easy interval language while playing. Teachers will also find that they can help the students achieve accurate reading skills in a very short time, by allowing the teacher to know what the student is thinking. The student will also, have to be clear on the interval perceived, before transferring the message to the fingers, so guesswork is eliminated. A demonstration of this appears in the Contemporary Piano Method DVD

Sing the number 'one' for the first note of each piece, and insert the counting between the intervals for longer notes.
For instance: *Sing*

4/4	1	Step up	Step up	Step up	Step up	2	3	4
	Skip down	2	Skip down	2	Step up	Step up	Skip down	2	off

Integrated support materials for this level

Aural   ★ *Contemporary Aural Course: Preparatory Set*   **Theory**   ★ *Contemporary Theory Primer*

Practical   ★ *Contemporary Piano Method DVD*

      ★ *Junior Trax* - This book contains familiar tunes arranged for two hands using continuous movement, with very few rests, so that the interval reading can develop by touch. Commence these tunes after completing page 45. Once the Junior Primer has been completed, they can be played with hands together.

      ★ *Guide Notes for Teachers:* An abbreviated guide appears on the final pages of this book. An expanded version appears on my website: **www.margaretbrandman.com**

Margaret Brandman
Ph.D. (Music/Arts) HonDL., B.Mus., A.Mus.A., DipE (WPTA)
T.Mus.A., ASA T.Dip., F.Mus.Ed.ASMC., F.Comp.ASMC., L. Perf.ASMC.

SECTION ONE - The Basics

Seating Position

Look inside the piano to see the hammers and the strings

Sit towards the front edge of the chair

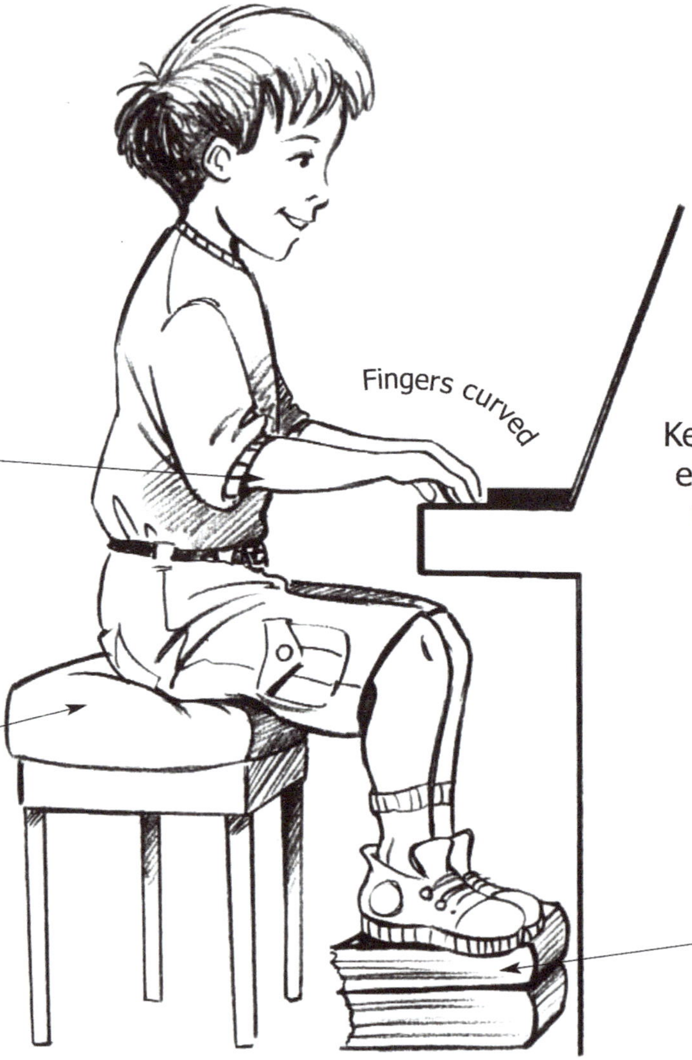

Keep elbows a few inches away from the side of the body

Fingers curved

Keep the line from elbow to wrist at the same level

Add cushions to bring the elbow to the right height if needed

Place feet on a solid box or foot-stool, or old phone books to provide balance and support

What type of piano or keyboard do you play?

Grand Piano

Upright Piano

Electronic Keyboard

Hand Position

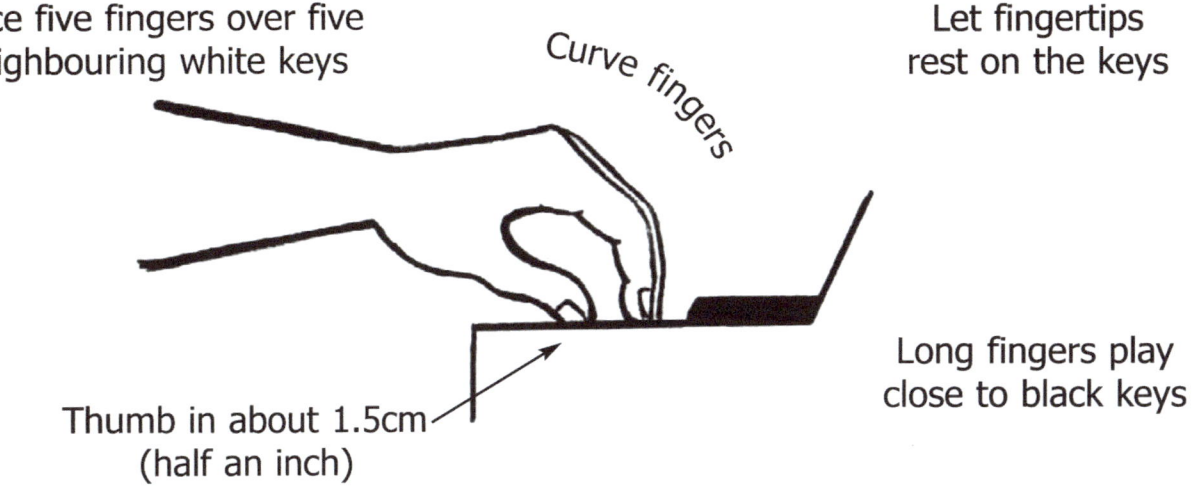

Place five fingers over five neighbouring white keys

Curve fingers

Let fingertips rest on the keys

Thumb in about 1.5cm (half an inch)

Long fingers play close to black keys

Finger Numbers

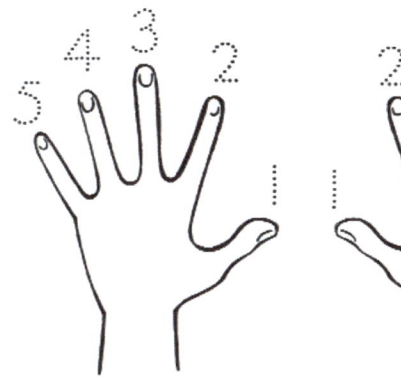

Trace the numbers in blue pencil

Trace the numbers in red pencil

Teacher Student Game:
Point required finger using either left or right hand.

How To Play:

★ First balance the arm weight while holding down all five neighbouring keys. The shape of your hand should look like an arch.

★ Now balance weight on the *middle finger only*.

★ Next play finger 2 by first *lifting* your curved finger and then *dropping* it onto the key.

★ Let finger 3 'pop' off the key when the next note sounds.

★ Now play your thumb (finger 1) then play all the other fingers: 2, 3, 4 and 5 and then in reverse. Remember to lift and then drop.

Keyboard Geography

The Piano Keyboard

Here is a picture of the piano keyboard.
Notice how the black notes are arranged in groups of two or three.

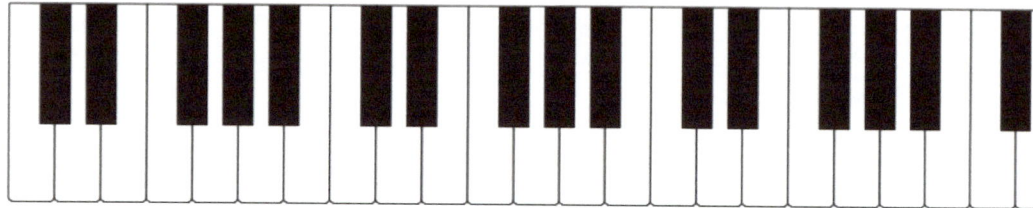

creativity corner

Invent some musical sounds using only the black notes, for example:

a) call and response - teacher and student

b) musical conversations - Left Hand answered by Right Hand

c) make up some songs to words about the interesting things in your life

d) use the entire length of the piano to hear the low, middle and high sounds

Two Important Signpost Notes

Meet 'Dexter' the koala

 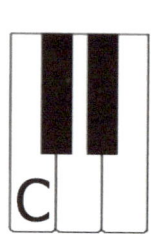  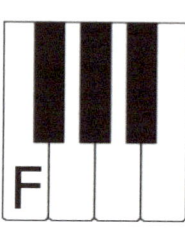

The other notes are named according to the letters of the alphabet. In music we only use seven letters: **A B C D E F G**
Here they are on one section of the keyboard: *fill in the other names*

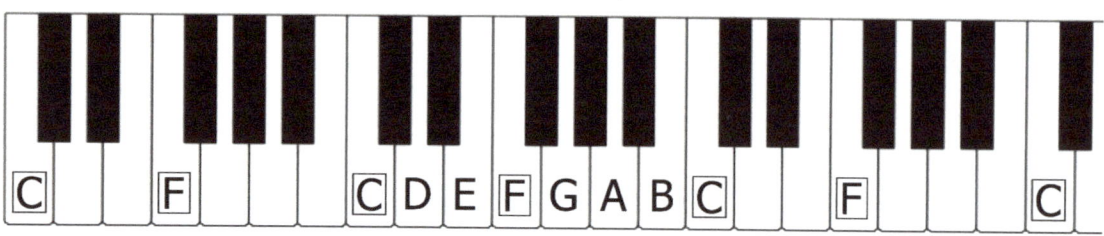

For extra writing see: Contemporary Theory Primer p5

Colour all the C's in red pencil and all the F's in green

8

Match these pictures to find the signpost notes with your
Right Hand thumb and Left Hand fifth finger

Then close your eyes and let your hands travel along the length of the keyboard, from the lowest to the highest sounds, feeling for the groups of black notes and sounding the C's and F's

Say the names of the notes aloud as you play them

Feel the keys!

Right Hand C 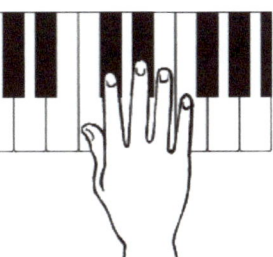   Right Hand F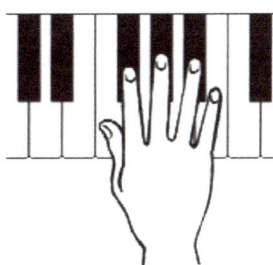

Left Hand C 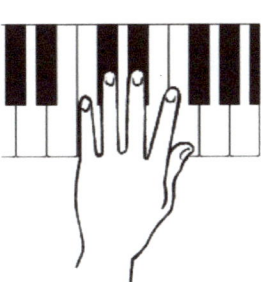   Left Hand F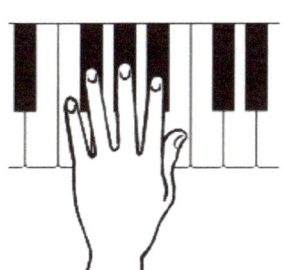

Signpost Notes

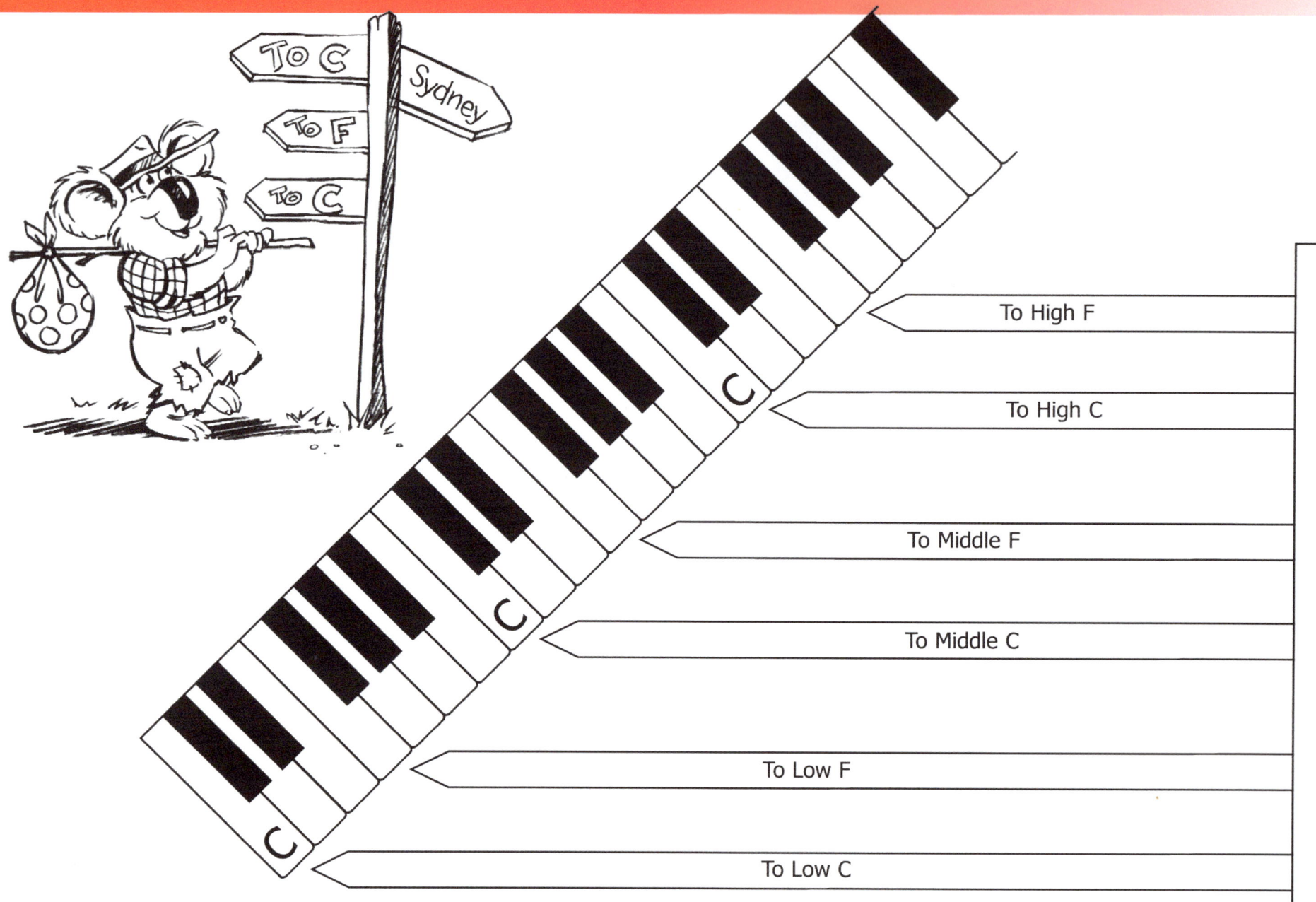

Notes On The Staff

The Staff or Stave is the set of *five lines* and *four spaces* on which music is written

A Staff

Trace the numbers

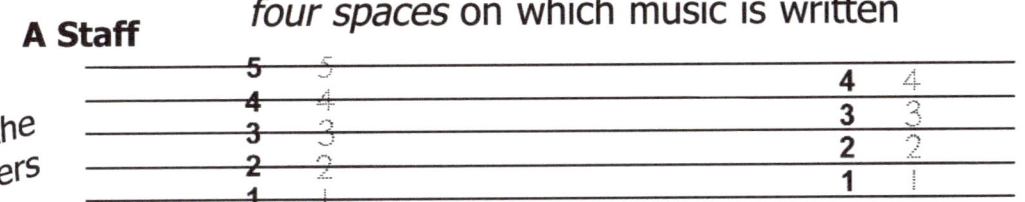

The lines and spaces are numbered from bottom to top

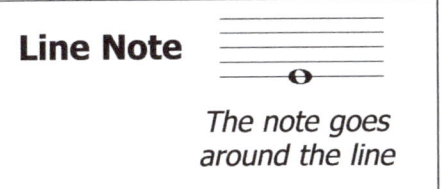

Line Note — The note goes around the line

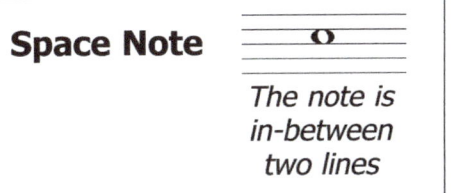

Space Note — The note is in-between two lines

Leger Lines

Extra lines for musical sounds

Leger Line Space Notes: Leger Line Line Notes:

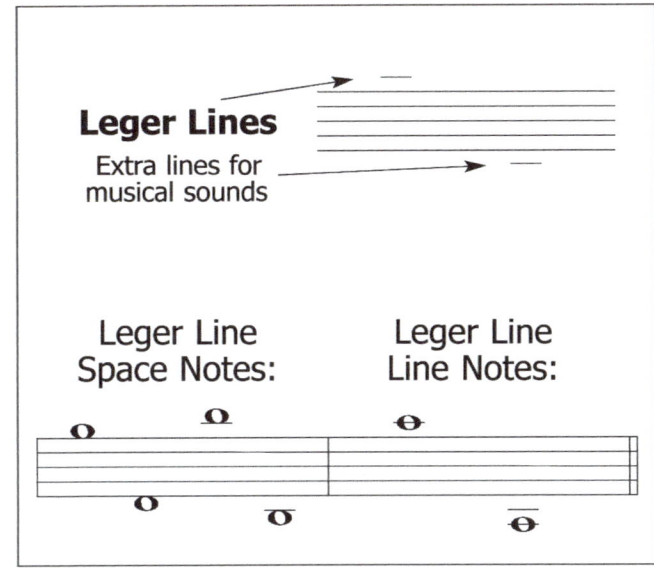

1. Copy these:

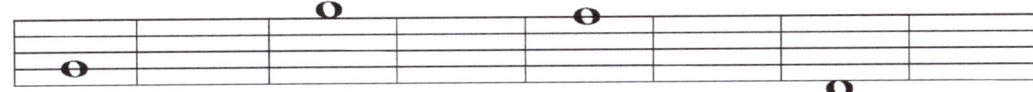

2. Line Notes or Space Notes? (L or S)

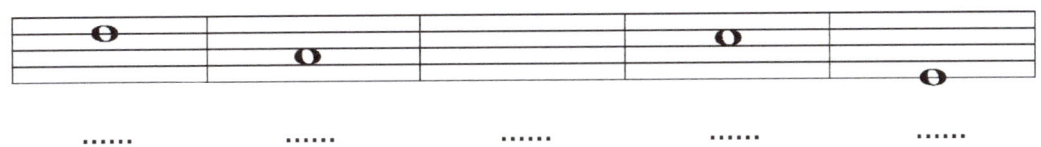

…… …… …… …… ……

3. Draw Line Notes:

4. Draw Space Notes:

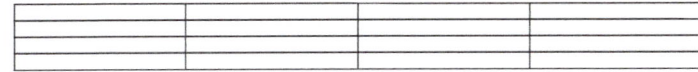

11

A Musical Map

Copy Dexter's actions while your teacher sounds *high*, *middle* and *low* notes

High and Low Sounds

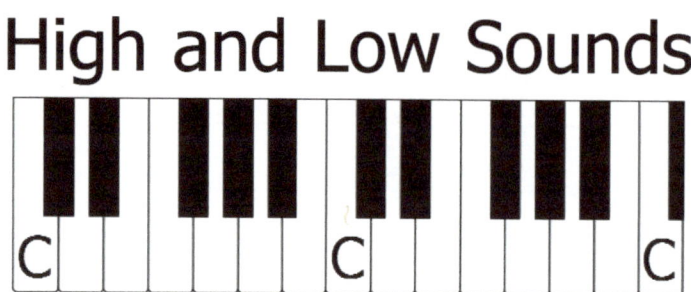

What animal or bird sounds can you make at the *high* end of the keyboard?

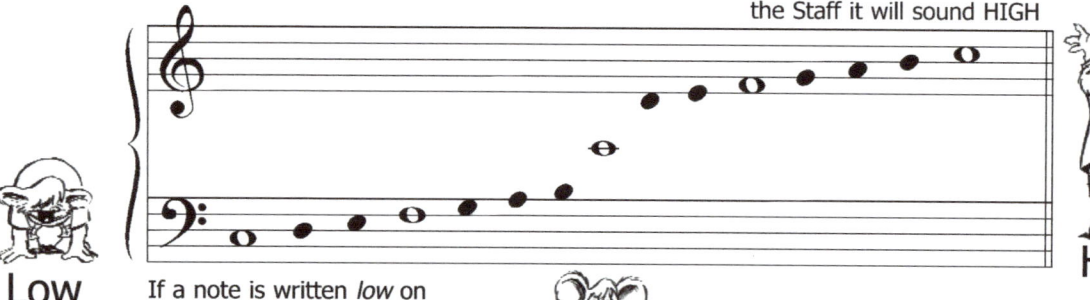

What animal sounds can you make at the *low* end of the keyboard?

Quick Quiz

1. Tick the *highest* note of each group:

2. Tick the *lowest* note of each group:

Colour Dexter's shirts: Low - dark blue, Middle - red, High - yellow

Refer to:

Contemporary Theory Primer p7

For listening see:

Aural Course Preparatory Lesson 1

Exploring Low, Middle and High Sounds

1. Make up two songs following the low, middle or high pictures of Dexter. You can choose notes all along the keyboard from the *lowest* to the *highest*, or play them all in one hand position, using fingers one, three and five.

2. Play five *low* notes moving *up*   and   Play five *high* notes moving *down*

Left Hand

Right Hand

3. Play *middle* notes

Right Hand

Start with thumbs on Middle C

Left Hand

Things to practise after your first lesson:
★ Playing five finger groups of notes in stepwise fashion
★ Finding C's and F's - high and low
★ Improvise on the black notes
★ Creative work on this page

13

Getting to Know the Music Ladder & Intervals

An interval is the distance from one note to the next. Here are three of them:

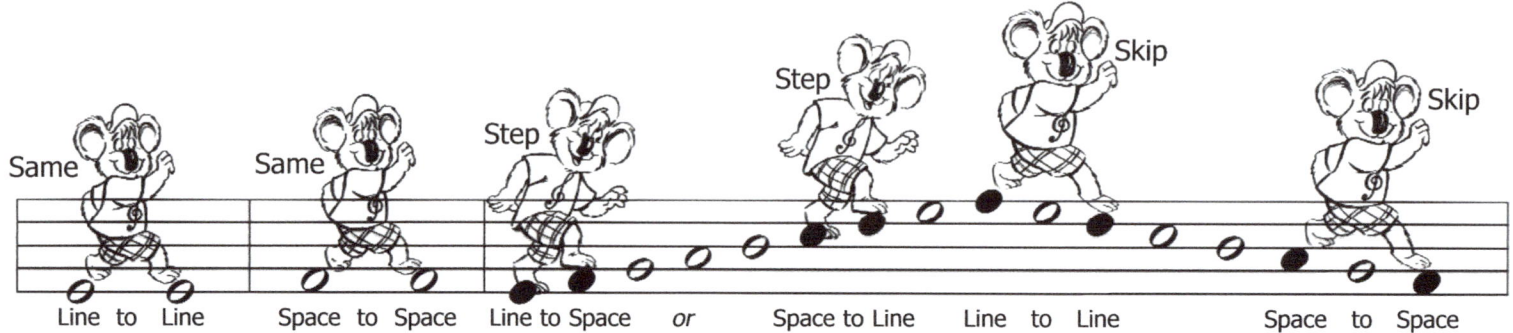

Look - Feel - Play and Listen to Intervals
Start on any key you wish with either the thumb (Right Hand) or the fifth finger (Left Hand)

Play Sames
Use the same finger twice. Looks, feels and sounds the same.

Say 'SAME' for the second note

Play Steps
Walk your fingers! Use one finger per note. Can you hear the music rise and fall?

Say '1-STEP UP', 'STEP UP' or 'STEP DOWN' as you play the notes

Play Skips
Skip a key and skip one finger. A skip sounds a little further away than a step.

Say 'SKIP' as you play the notes

Refer to: Contemporary Theory Primer pp 8&9

Preparatory Lesson 3 and Lesson 5 Part A

Colour Dexter's Shirts: Same - red, Step Up - green, Skip Up - yellow, Skip Down - orange

Feeling Intervals

Touch These!
Place your finger-tips on these notes

For *Steps* - you need one finger for each one

Line Space Line Space Line

Think of the notes as the ends of your fingertips, as if you had drawn a circle around each one.

Skips

For *Skips* - you leave out one finger

Line Line *or* Space Space

Practical Activities:
1) Play the interval Drill Game with your teacher
2) Compose / Improvise your own songs using Sames, Steps and Skips
3) Ask your teacher to record your performance

★ Something Extra ★
Find three steps near your house and climb them while singing *Step-up*, or *Skip-down*, or *Same*

Activity Page - Writing Intervals

Compare these:

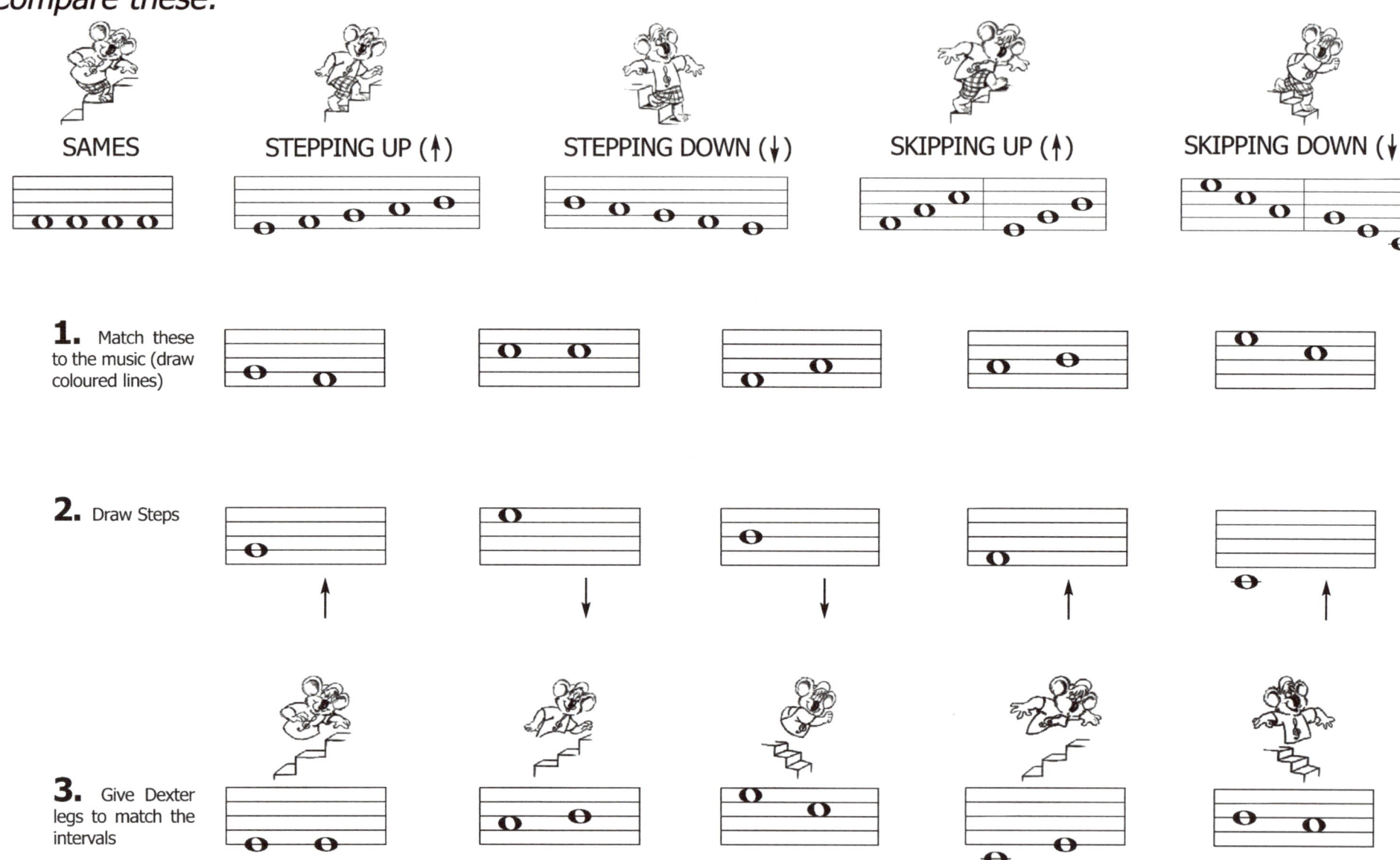

Colour Dexter's Shirts: Same - red, Step Up - green, Step Down - Blue, Skip Up - yellow, Skip Down - orange

A Picture Song to Play

Rhythm in Music

Notes represent sounds

Each note has a different shape to show how long the sound continues. They can be named in two ways.

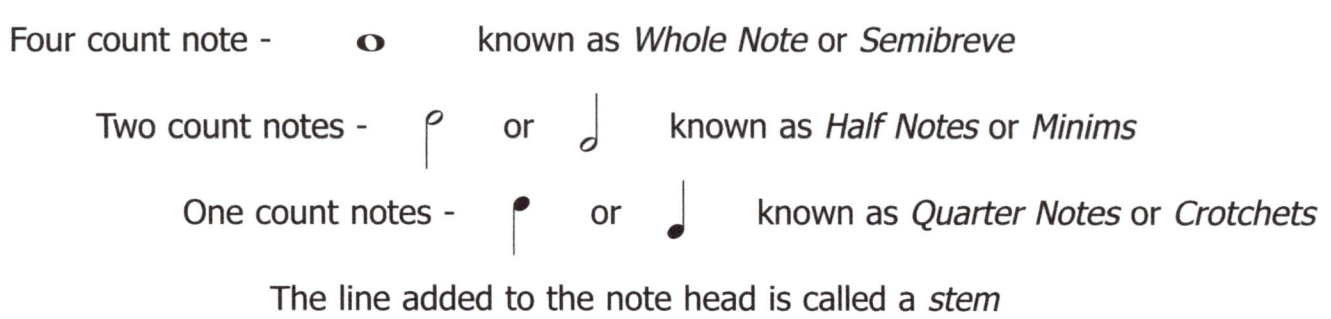

The line added to the note head is called a *stem*

Rests represent silence

Each note has a matching rest which shows how long the silence continues.

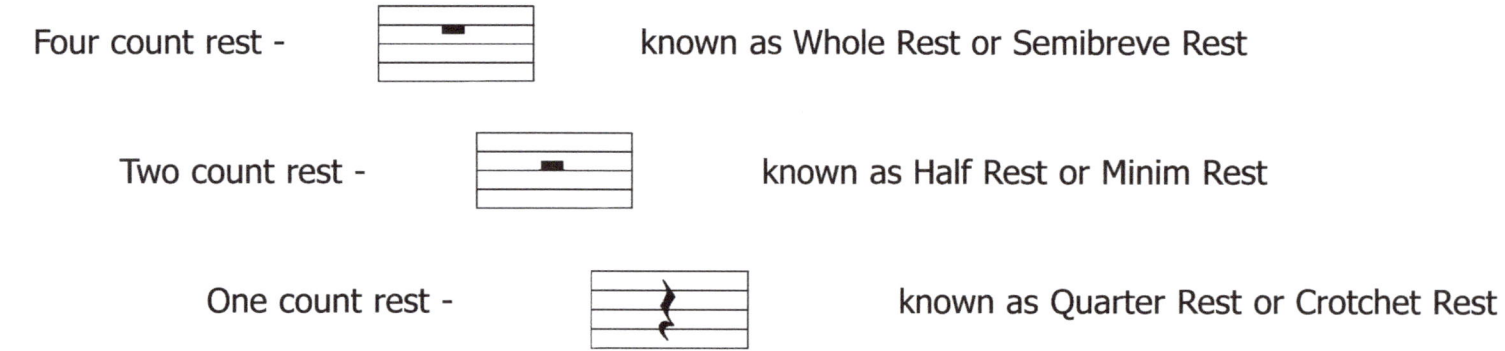

Rhythm Quiz

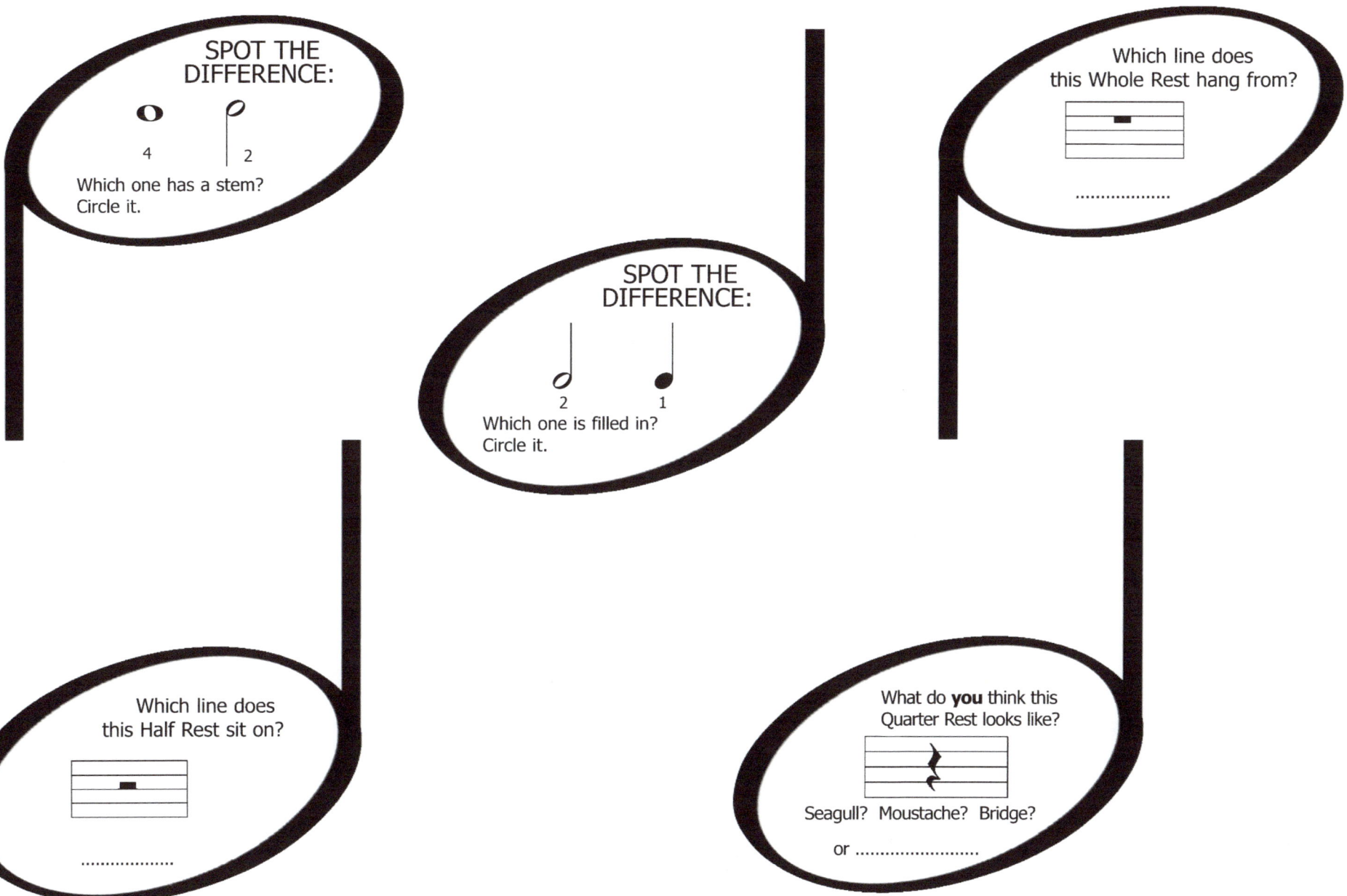

Colour & Clap - Colour Chart

Colour in the boxes to match the back cover of this book

Notes:

Note	Colour
whole note (1 2 3 4)	mauve and/or purple
half note (1 2)	yellow and/or orange
quarter note (1)	dark blue and/or light blue

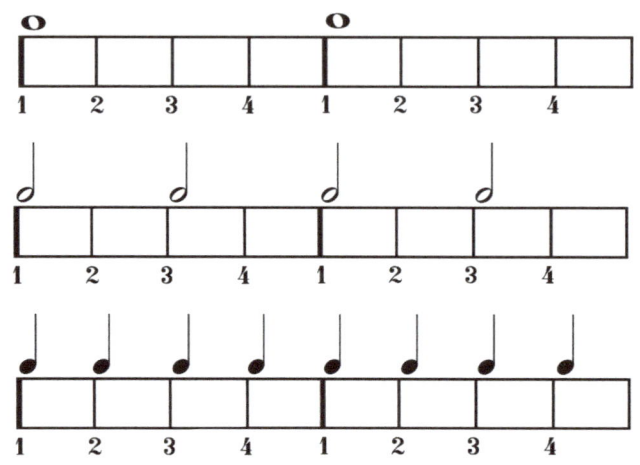

> **Notes...**
> represent sounds to be played, clapped or sung.

Rests:

whole rest (1 2 3 4)	leave blank
half rest (1 2)	leave blank
quarter rest (1)	leave blank

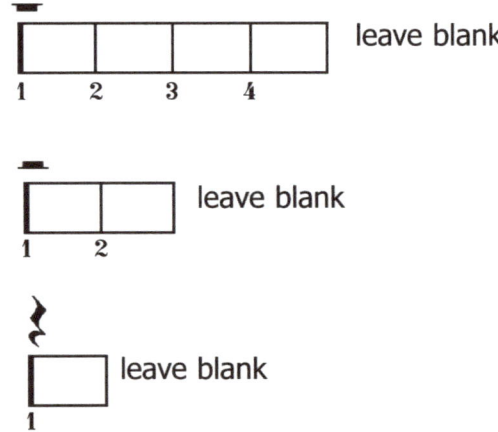

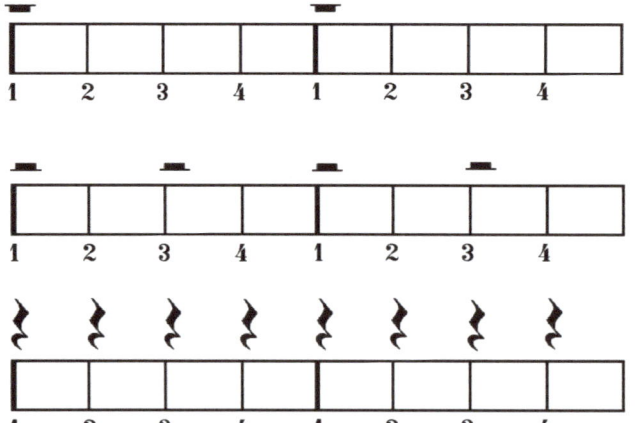

> **Rests...**
> represent periods of silence.
> Stop playing, just keep counting!

Activity Page - Colour & Clap

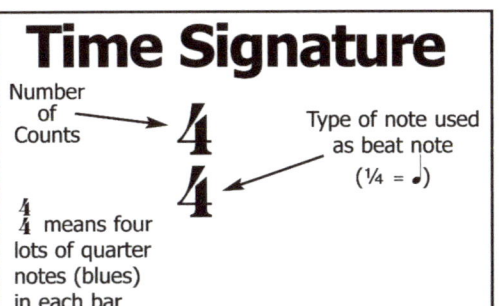

Time Signature

Number of Counts → 4
Type of note used as beat note (¼ = ♩) ← 4

4/4 means four lots of quarter notes (blues) in each bar

Colour & Clap

Colour in the boxes and clap the time values

★ Hold hands together while the colour continues
★ For rests - take hands apart and beat time in the air

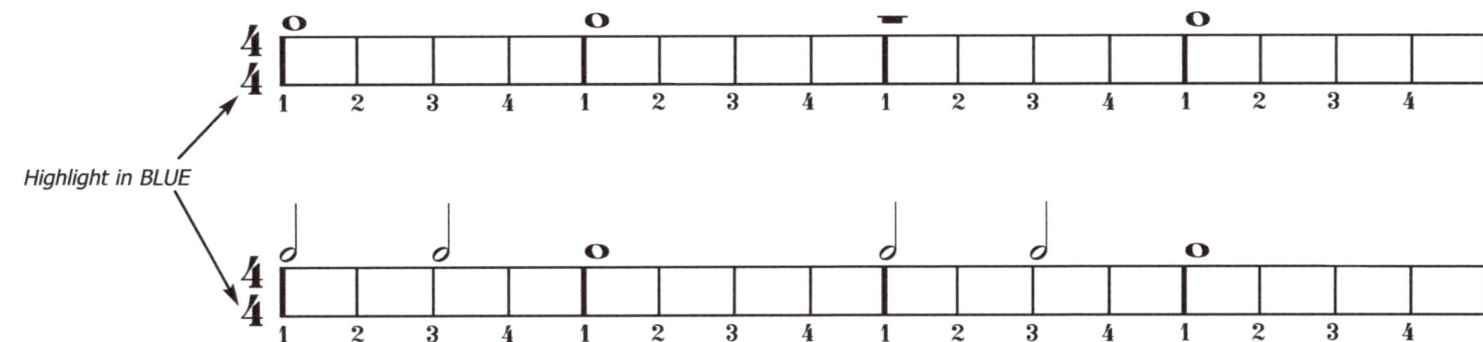

Highlight in BLUE

Look at the *top* number of the time signature to see *how many* counts in each bar

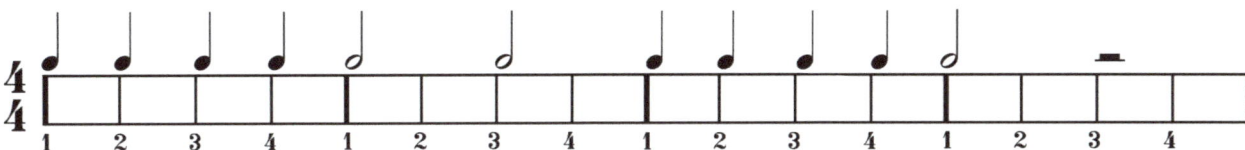

Clap the rhythms to tracks 3&4 from *Rhythm Unravelled (Book and Audio)* by Kerin Bailey

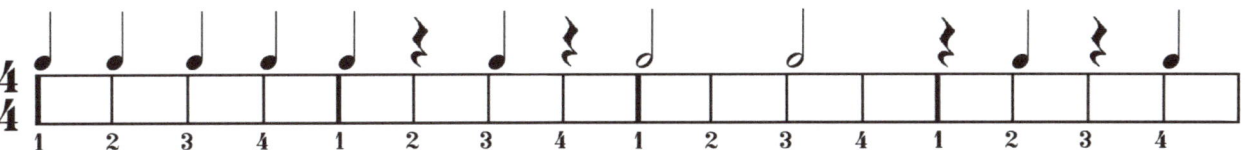

The Great Staff and Middle C

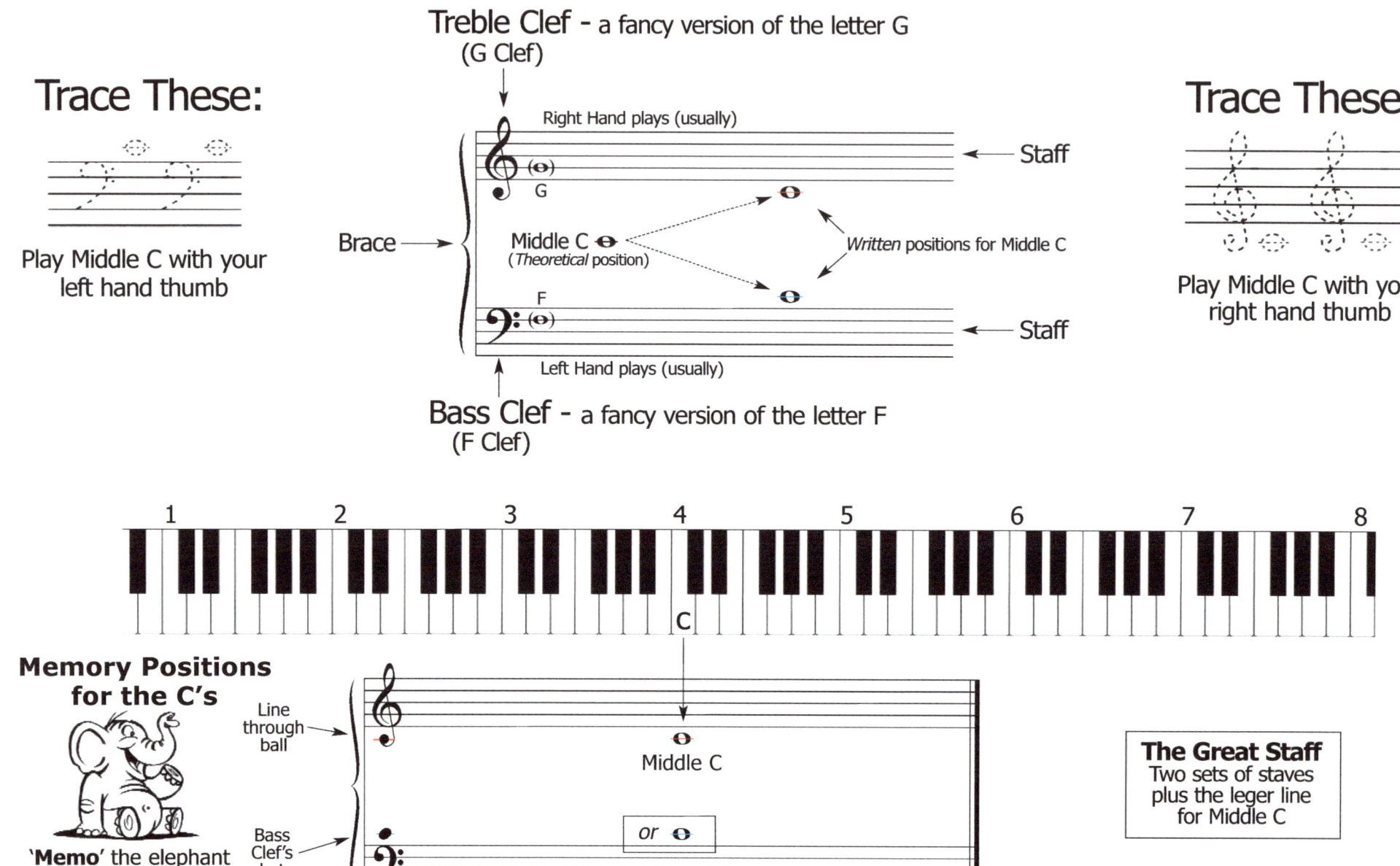

Improvising

1) Play some steps, skips and sames with your Right Hand .... 𝄞

   Play some steps, skips and sames with your Left Hand .... 𝄢

2) Follow the clefs to play a few notes in each hand to make your own song. Begin with Right Hand on High C and Left Hand on Low C using any finger.

3) Hands together easily: Play some steps using mirror fingers, starting either on both thumbs or both fifth fingers on Low C and High C. Say the combined direction when hands play together: Out or In

Single Bar Lines
Upright lines are used to divide the music into bars or measures

Bar / Bar Line / Bar or Measure

Double Bar Lines
The double lines show the end of the music

Double Bar Line

Things To Do after Lesson Two:

★ Play the interval drill game

★ Improvise on black or white notes

★ Play *Ode To Joy*

★ Colour & Clap - p21

★ Improvising on p23 using clefs

DAILY WARM-UP: Play the music following the clef cues with mirror fingers for several weeks after it is learnt.
COMBINED DIRECTIONS: Refer to Contemporary Theory Primer p8

SECTION TWO - Reading & Playing Steps & Sames

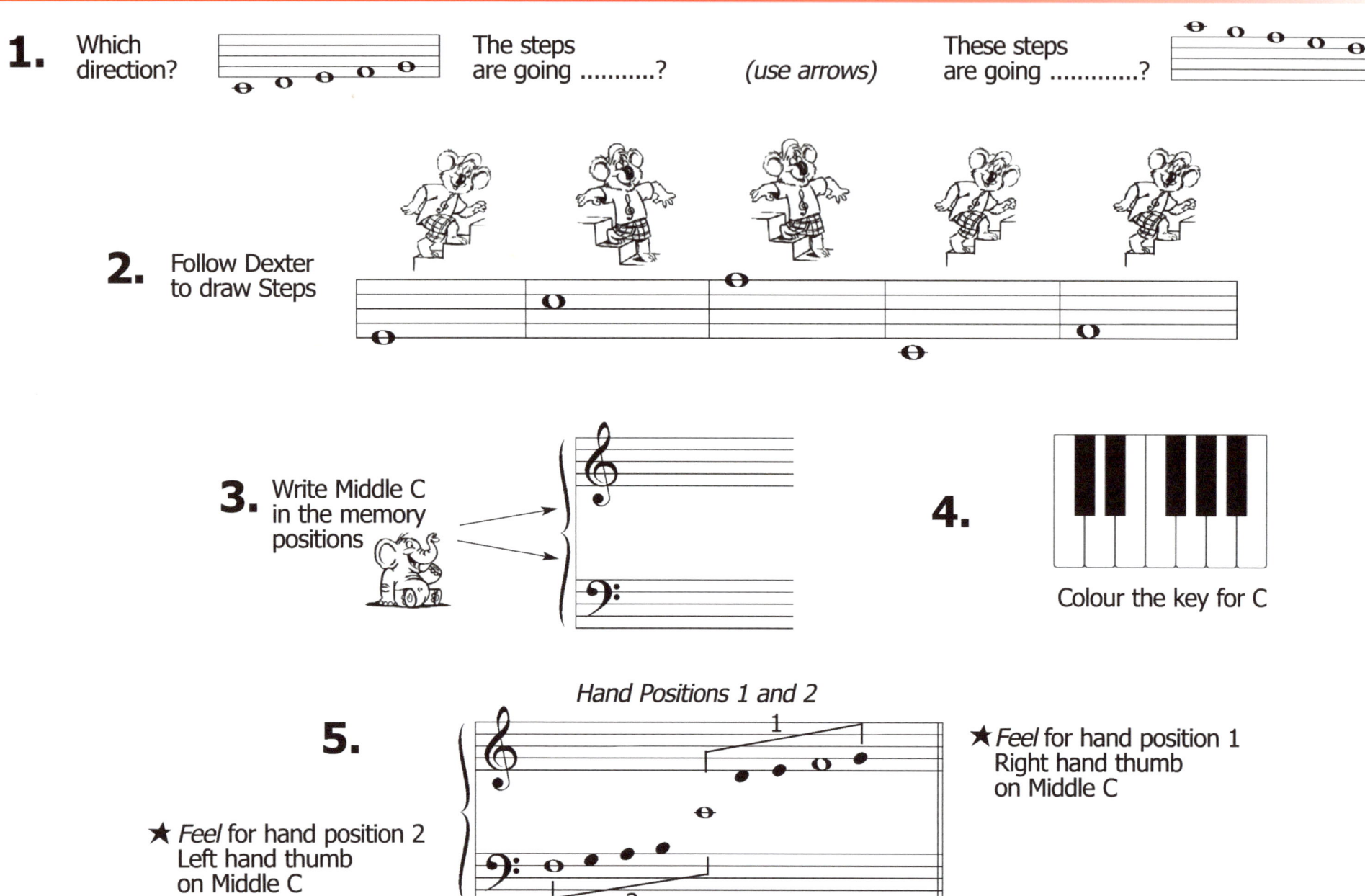

Follow The Flow

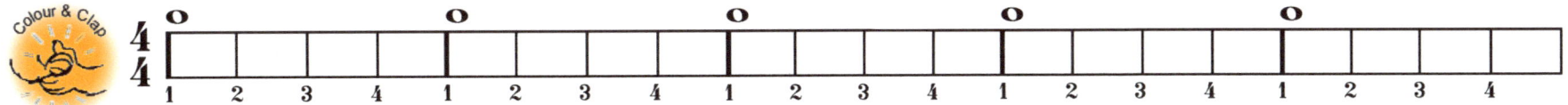

Reading, Feeling, Playing and Listening to Steps

Use the *playing made easy* system to play this music:

1) Finger-trace the music to feel the direction and the intervals
2) Talk/Sing the interval and direction when you see the asterisk *
3) Speed learning playing package: talk/sing the combination of intervals, direction and counting

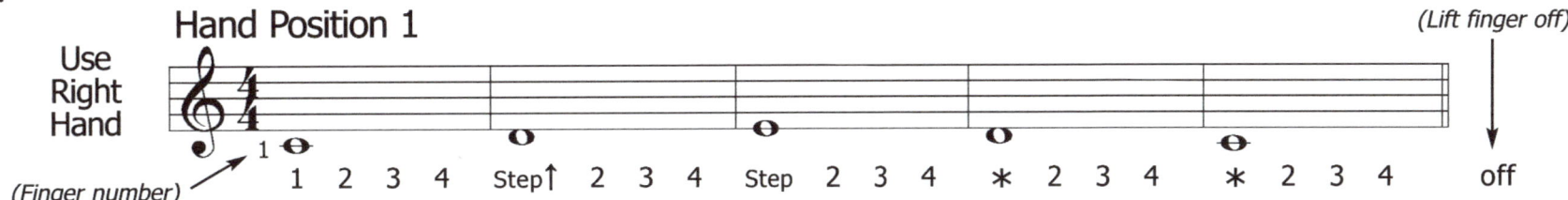

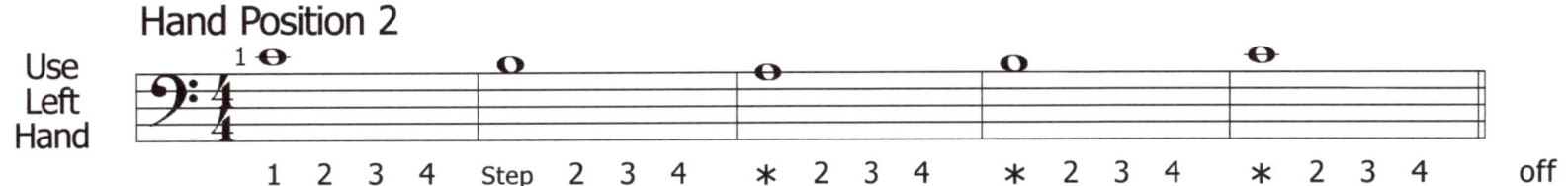

Preparatory Lesson 4 Question 1

Special Note: For every piece of music in this book, write the nearest Signpost C to the printed starting note. Write each C in its memory position using the given colour.

Write and Play Steps

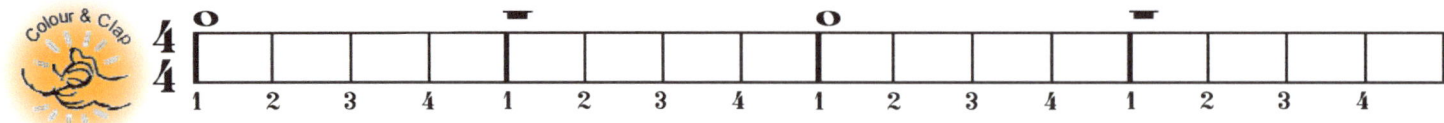

★ Write and play
Use four-count notes

The See-Saw Song

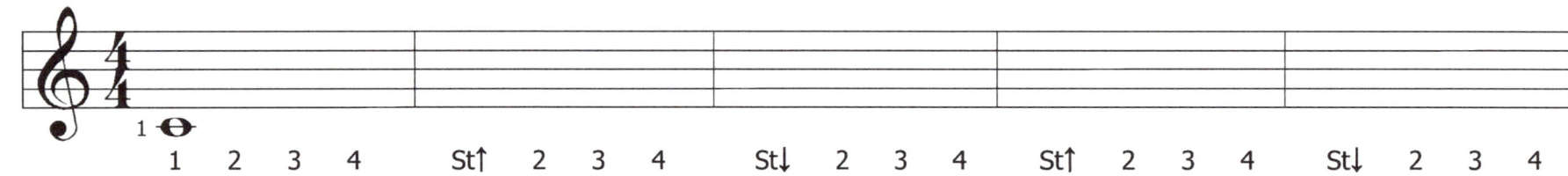

Finger Numbers

Write numbers above fingers

Improvising:
Make up a short tune using steps, for either hand or both hands together. Can you make contrasting sounds, by sounding the notes very loud or very softly?
What funny sounds can you make, by playing the steps with both notes at once?

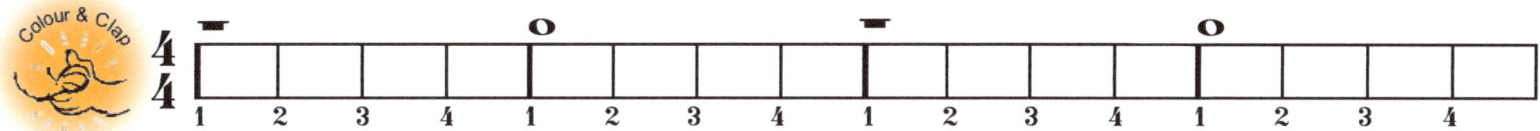

Quick Quiz

Going *up* ↑ or going *down* ↓ ?

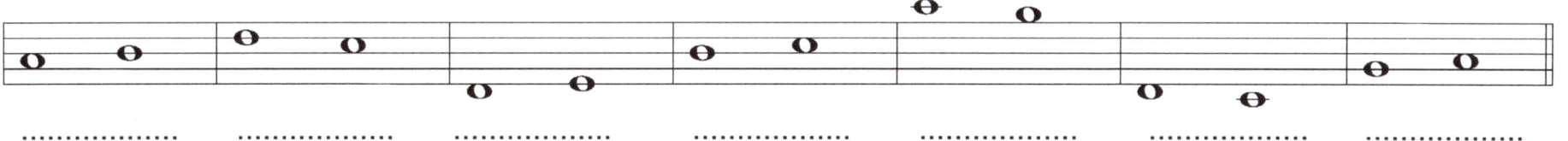

....

Wiggling Steps

Follow Dexter to write and play Use four-count notes

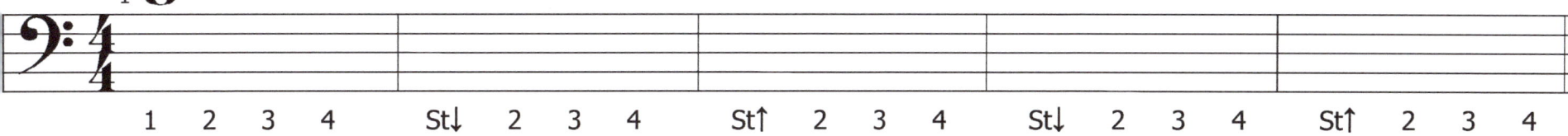

Signpost C's

Colour Code all the C's

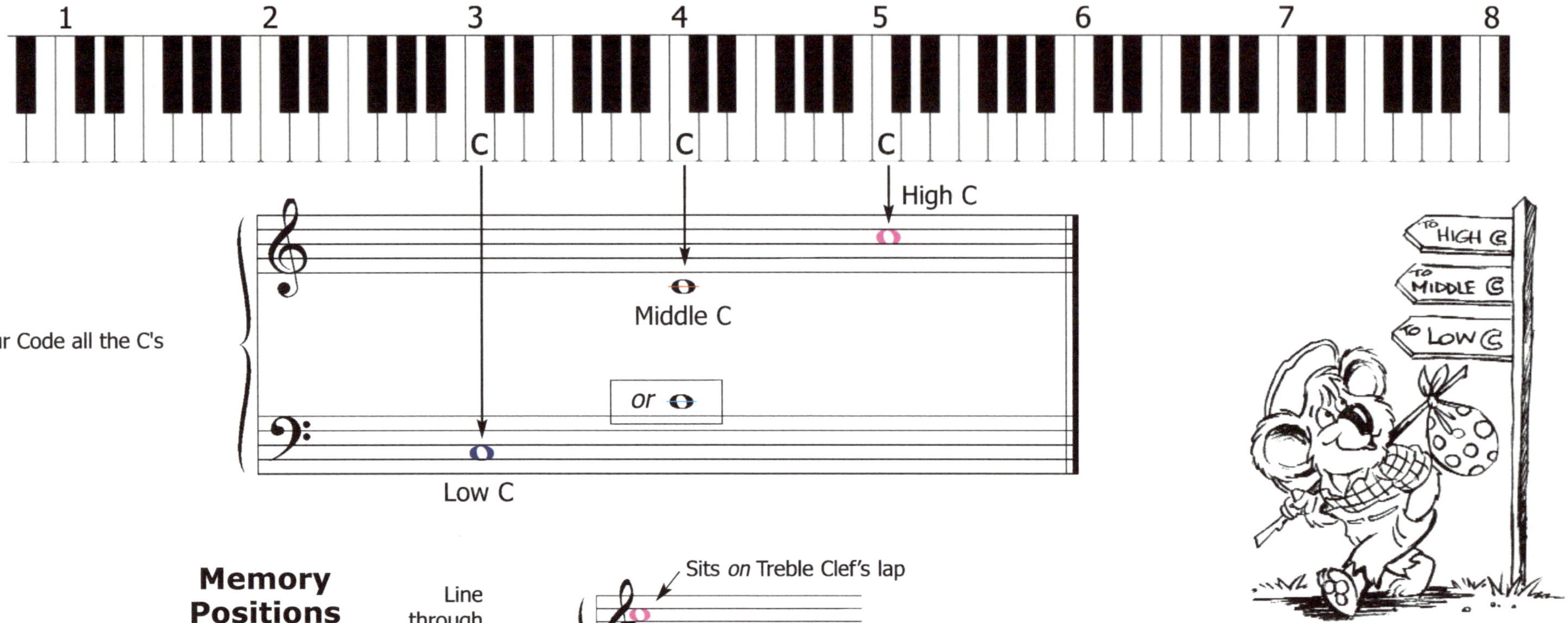
1
2
3
4
5
6
7
8
C
C
C
High C
Middle C
or
Low C
TO HIGH C
TO MIDDLE C
TO LOW C

Memory Positions for the C's

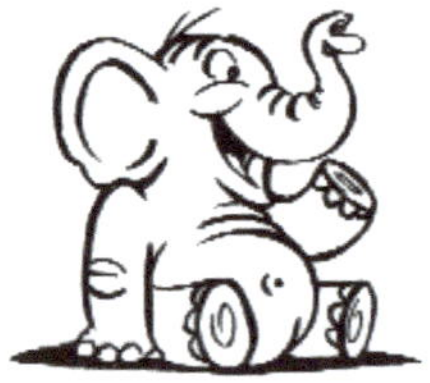

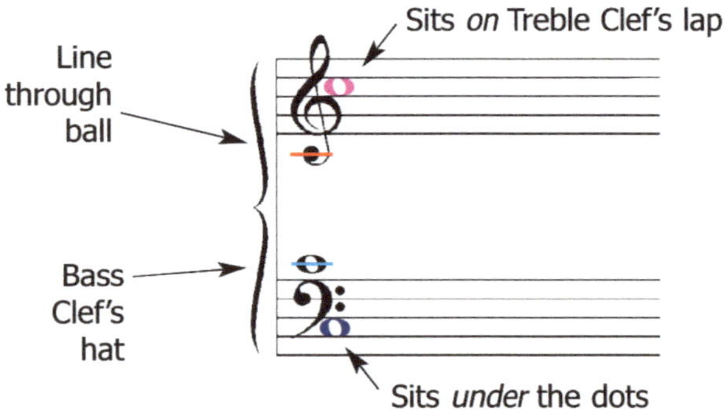
Sits *on* Treble Clef's lap
Line through ball
Bass Clef's hat
Sits *under* the dots

Draw C's in their memory positions in colour

creativity corner

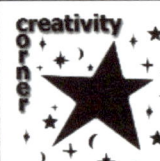

Improvising some C songs:

Improvise three rhythmic songs using only two notes. Use the rhythm unit from an electronic keyboard to provide an accompaniment to your 'C' songs.

a) Low C (LH) and Middle C (RH)

b) Middle C (LH) and High C (RH)

c) Low C (LH) and High C (RH)

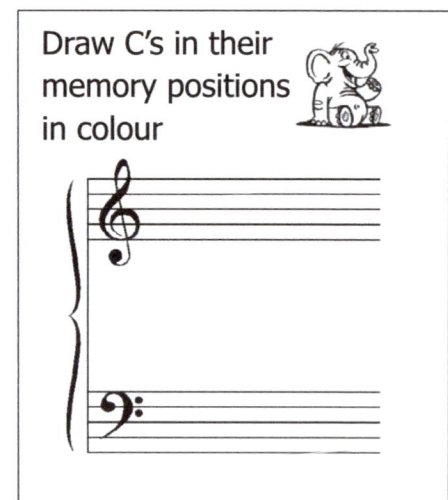

Follow The Flow From High & Low C

The 'Big Picture' for Hand Positions 3 and 4

Find these Hand Positions with your *eyes closed*! *Feel* for the Signpost Notes

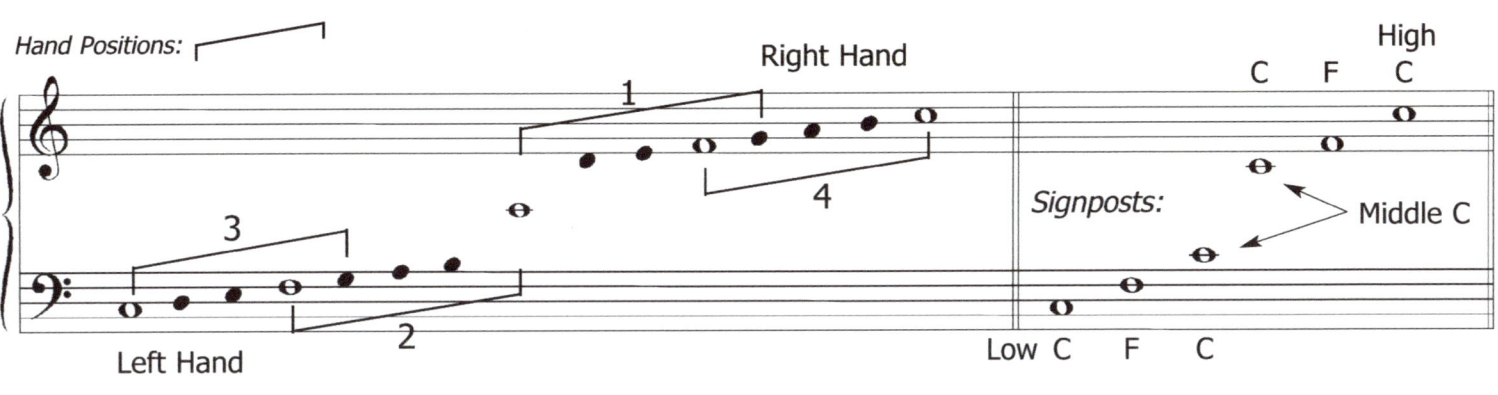

Follow The Flow
Play the duet from p25 with these two lines

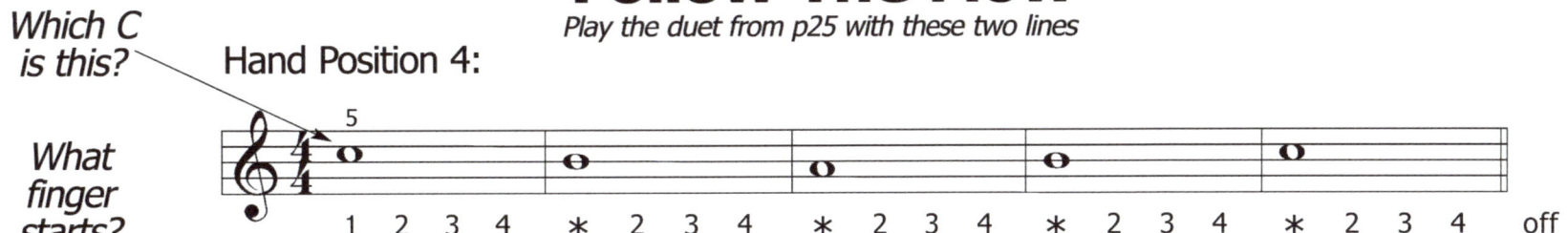

Prepare to play these lines of music by writing the Signpost C's in their memory positions.

Musical Shapes & Patterns: Similar Motion

Many musical shapes and patterns occur when hands play together
Similar Motion occurs when the music for both hands moves in the same *direction.*

Trace over the dotted lines with coloured pencils:

1. Notes for both hands moving down

2. Notes for both hands moving up

Practical Hint:
(as shown on the Contemporary Piano Method DVD)

⬅ Tilt your head to the *left* when the notes for both hands go *down*   Tilt your head to the *right* when the notes for both hands go *up* ➡

Stepping Easy - Up and Down
Talk/Sing intervals, direction, counting

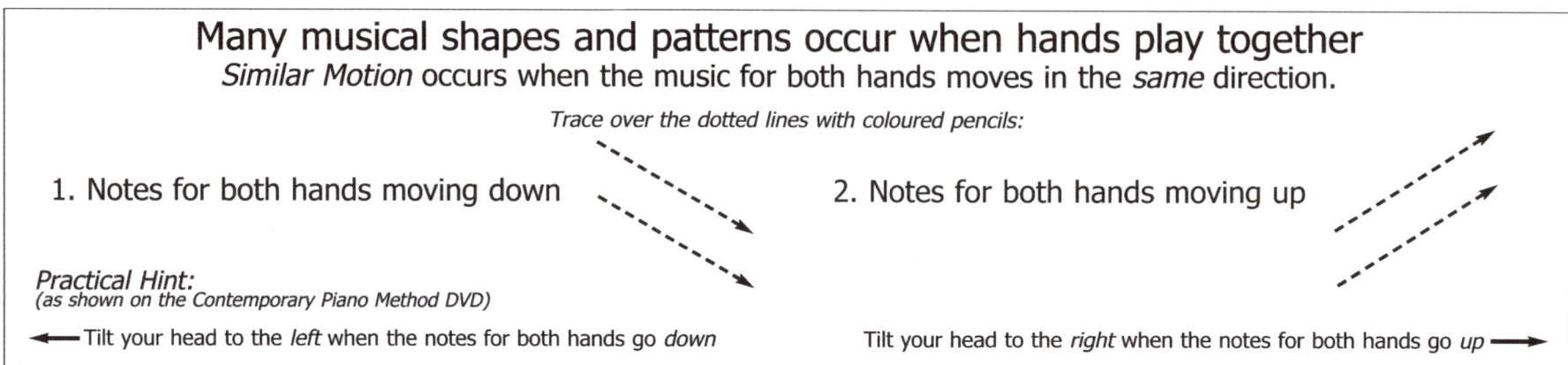

★ Focus on the lower line

H.P. 1

H.P. 3

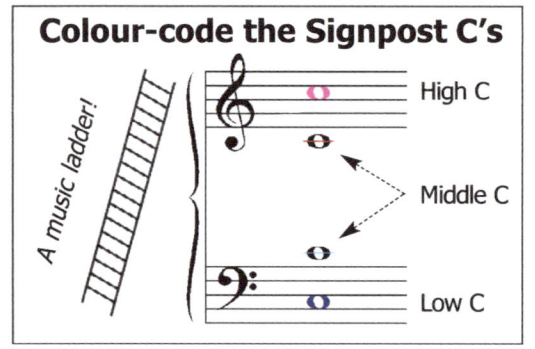

Colour-code the Signpost C's

High C

Middle C

Low C

A music ladder!

Teacher Duet:

Writing Activity

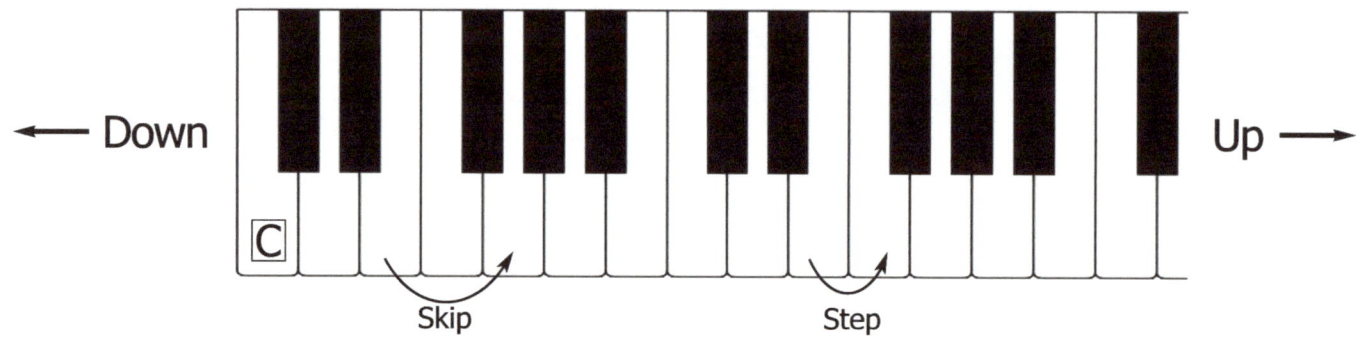

1. Write in the names of the signpost keys, C and F in *Red Pencil* on the picture of the keyboard
2. Write in the names of the other keys in ordinary pencil
3. Using arrows to help you work them out, name the keys that are:

   (1)   a *Step* up from C = ...
   (2)   a *Step* down from A = ...
   (3)   a *Skip* up from D = ...
   (4)   a *Skip* down from G = ...

   (5)   a *Step* down from B = ...
   (6)   a *Skip* up from F = ...
   (7)   a *Step* up from G = ...
   (8)   a *Skip* down from D = ...

1st: Intervals?
2nd: Note Names?

A Picture Song to Play

Can you guess its name?..

Sound the starting notes: O and follow with:

Preparation for playing:
1) *Colour Code* the koalas, by choosing one colour for each type
2) Both hands start a skip up from C, with the 3rd finger
3) Play separately and then together

2  steps↓   *then*   2  steps↑

2 sames   *then*

1  step↓   *and*   2  sames

1 step↑   *and*   2 sames

1 same   *and*   2  steps↓   *then*   2  steps↑

3  sames   *then*

1 step↓   *then*   1 same

1 step↑   *then*   2  steps↓

Look at page 44 for the words to sing with this song!

Play separately then together

33

Musical Shapes & Patterns: Contrary Motion

Contrary Motion occurs when the music moves in opposite direction

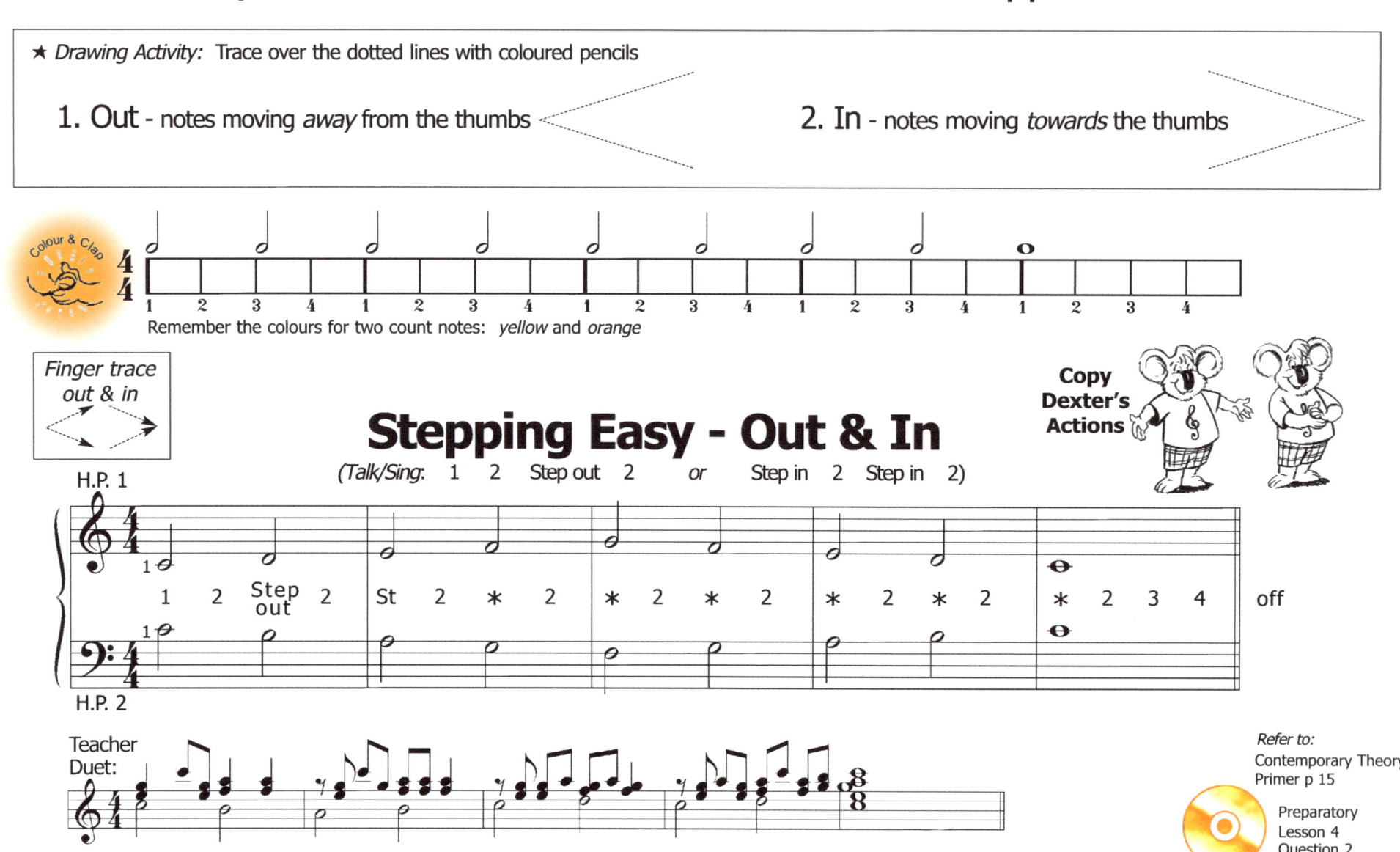

Trace the graphics: Orange for OUT and Purple for IN

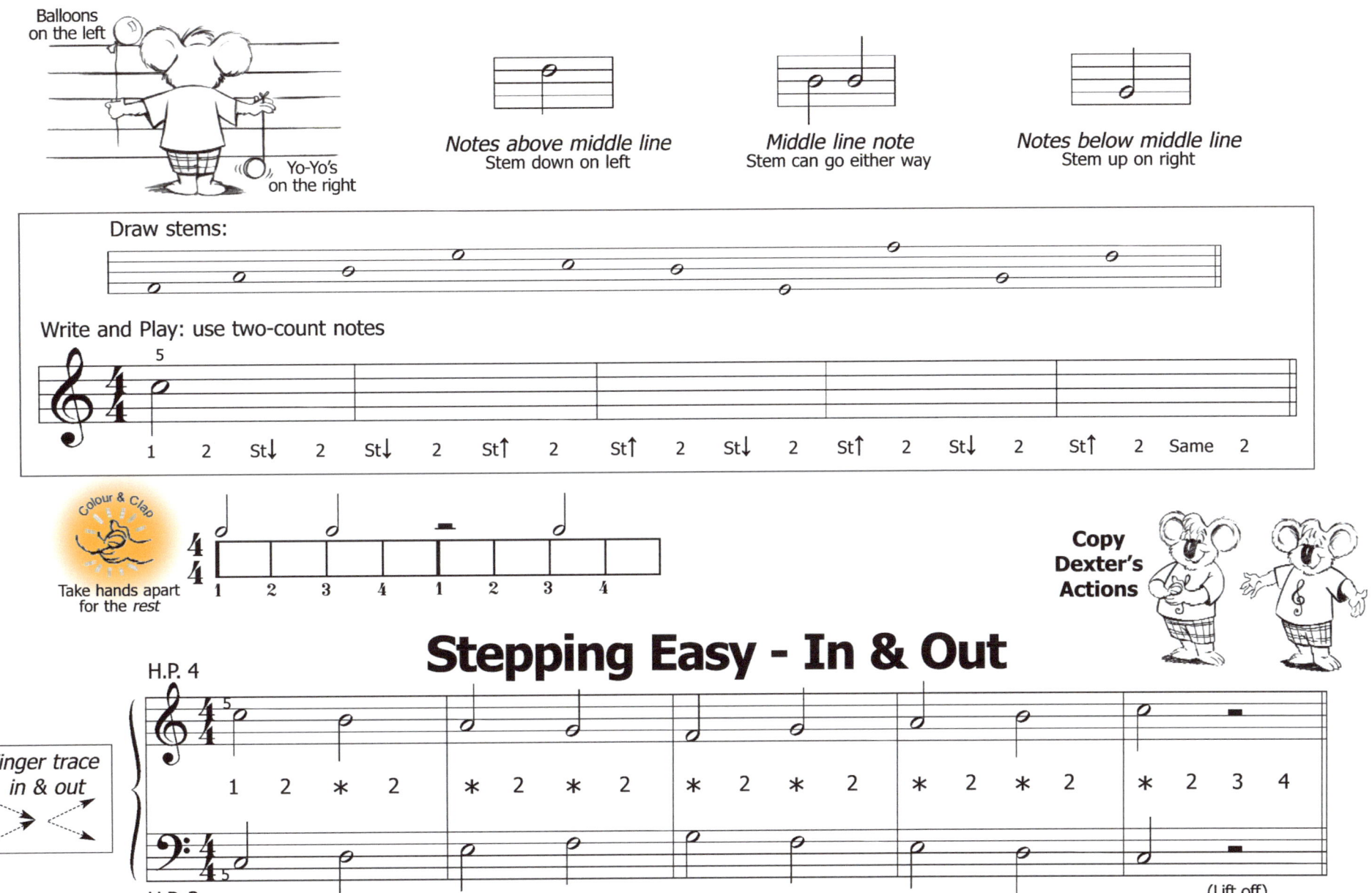

Playing Steps and Sames

A Picture Song to Play - Lightly Row

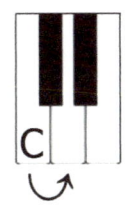

Prepare to play this piece by colour coding the Koalas.
Hold notes down for an extra beat when you see the short line ____
Call out the intervals as you play and say the word 'hold' when you see the line.
Start with Right Hand fifth finger on High D and Left Hand thumb one step up from Middle C.

Sound the starting notes: 𝐨 and follow with:

1 sk↓ then 1 same ____ 1 st↑ then 1 sk↓ and 1 same ____

1 st↓ then 4 st↑ and 2 sames ____

1 same then 1 sk↓ and 1 same ____ 1 st↑ and 1 sk↓ then 1 same

1 st↓ then 2 sk↑ then 1 same and 1 sk↓ _____ Long Hold

1 st↓ and 3 sames then 1 same and 2 st↑ ____

1 st↓ and 3 sames then 1 same and 2 st↑ ____

1 same and 1 sk↓ then 1 same ____ 1 st↑ and 1 sk↓ then 1 same

1 st↓ then 2 sk↑ then 2 sk↓ _____ Long Hold

The standard notation for this piece is presented on page 9 of *Dexter's Easy Piano Pieces* (also by Margaret Brandman)

Songs To Play

Draw Dexter's other foot on the staircase to match the intervals:

Song of Hills and Plains

Find the plains!   *Find the hills!*

Transpose begin on G

> **Accent**: Play the first beat in each bar *louder* than the others

Rain Is Falling Down

Repeat Sign — Play twice

Feel for G where is it?

How many skips?

Rain is fall-ing down ___ pit-ter pat-ter pit-ter pat-ter rain is fall-ing down ___

Hold

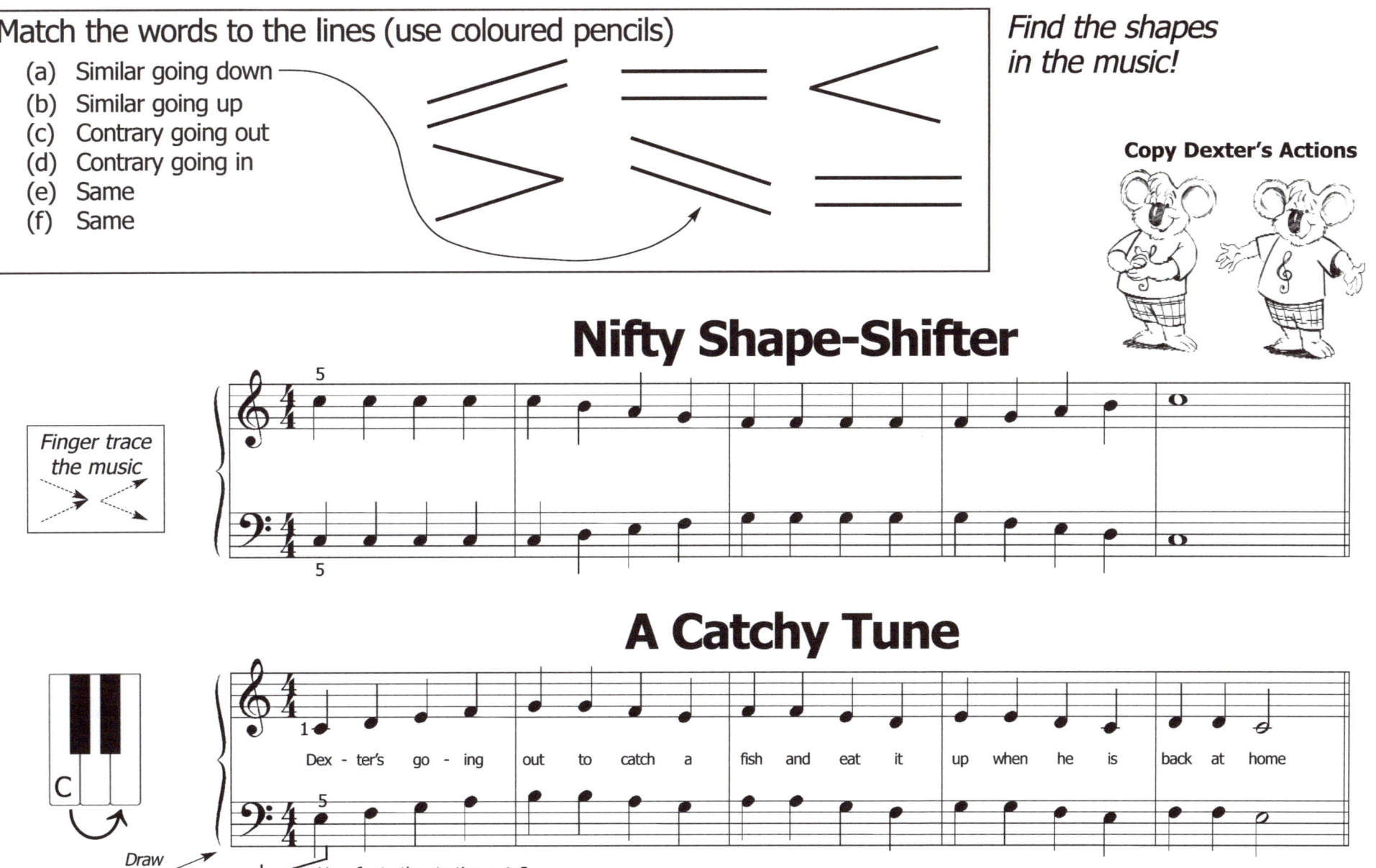

SECTION THREE - Reading & Playing Skips

Touch These!
Skip a Note / Skip a Finger

- ★ Play the Interval Drill Game
- ★ Use Mostly Skips

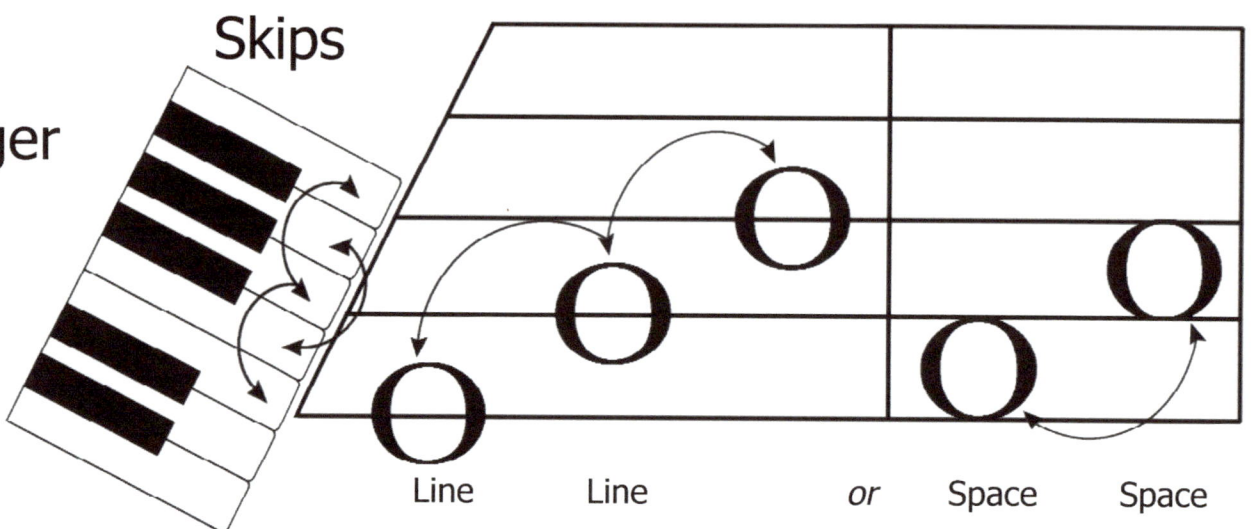

Skips

Line Line *or* Space Space

Write **Skips** up or down from the given notes:

Listen to the sound!

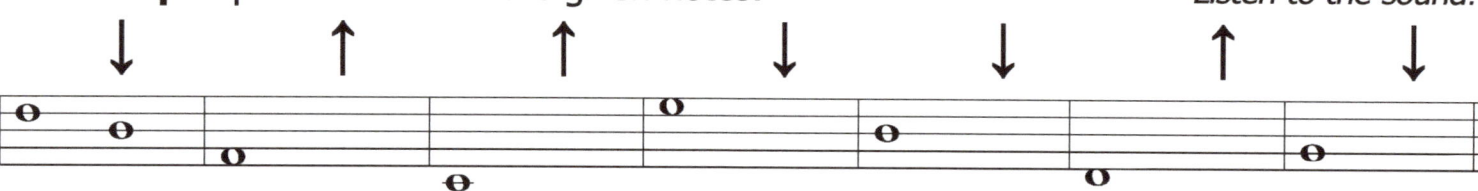

Circle the **Skips** in this line of music:

creativity corner — *Improvising* - Make up a short tune, using skips sounded at the same time. The sound of harmonic skips is very pleasant and sweet. You could play some long notes in the Left Hand, and find a tune that sounds well over these in the Right Hand.

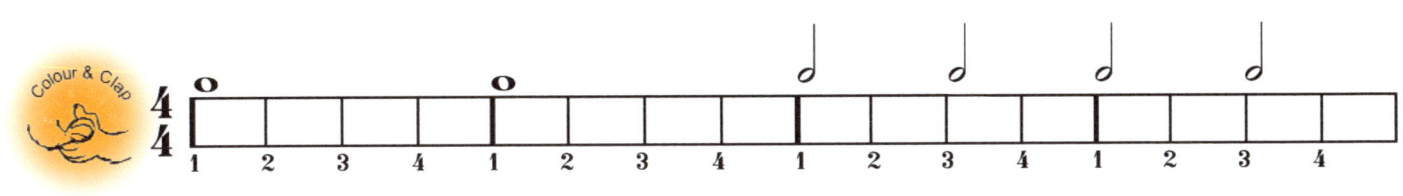

Memory Corner
Name these!

1. Before playing
2. and again while playing

Talk/Sing Intervals, Direction & Counting

Skipping Easy - Up & Down

Listen to the bright sound!

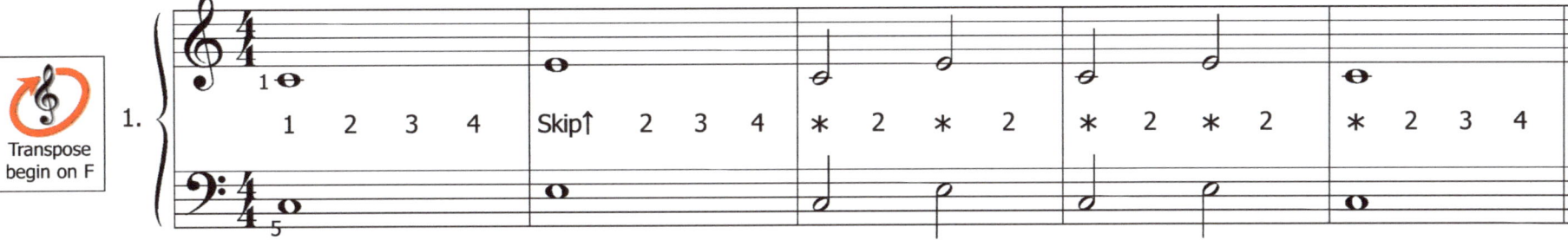

Transpose begin on F

Transpose begin on A

Listen to the sad sound!

Preparatory Lesson 5

41

More Skips To Play

Skipping Easy Round The Town
Skipping Easy Up & Down

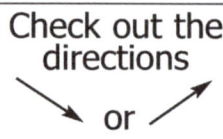
Check out the directions
↘ or ↗

Transpose begin on B

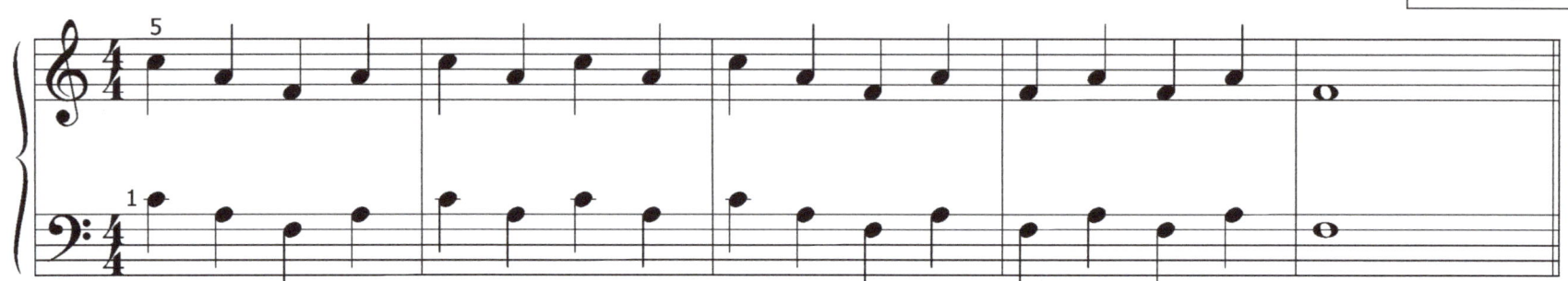

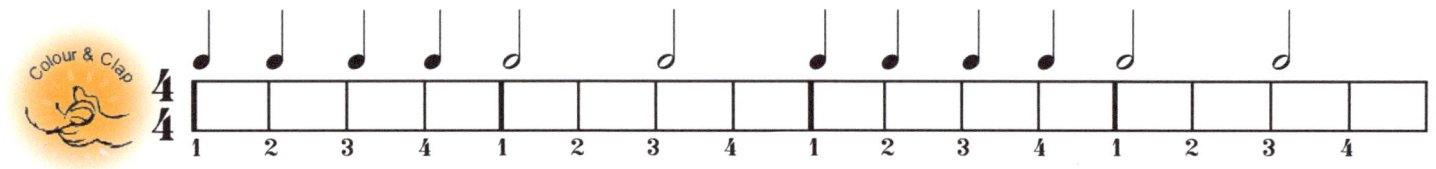
Colour & Clap

Fun With Skips

Transpose begin on D
Does it sound happy or sad?

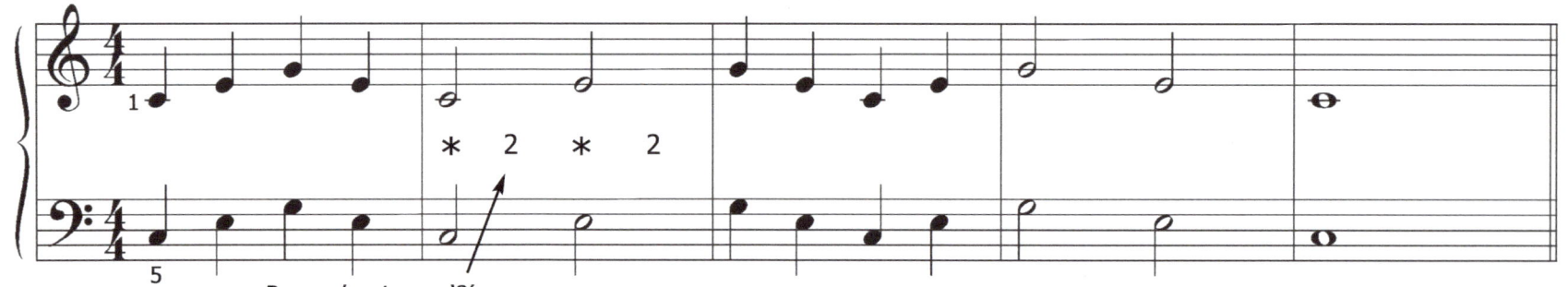

Remember to say '2'

★ *Something Extra:* play 'Rain Rain Go Away'

42

More Musical Shapes & Patterns

Another Nifty Shape-Shifter

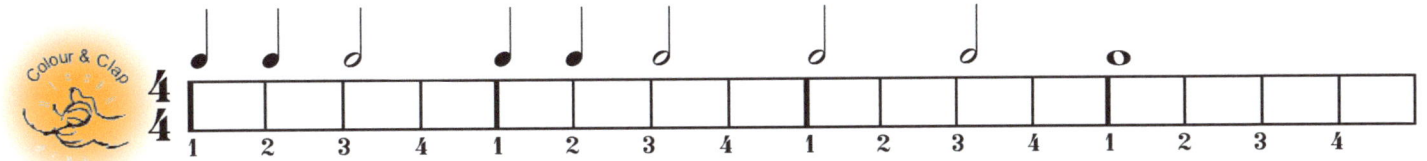

A Pretty Song of Steps & Sames

Can you spot the Skip?

Draw Low C

How far?

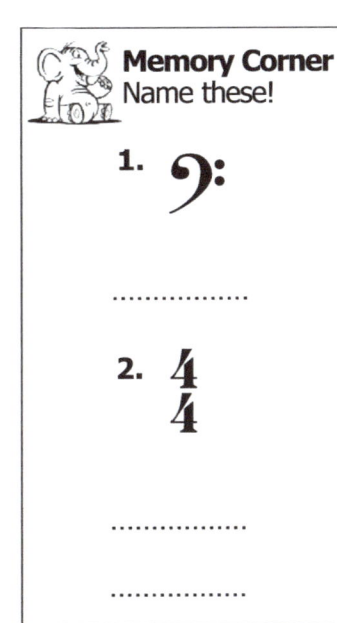

Memory Corner
Name these!

1.
2.

Longer Pieces of Music

Night-time Songs

A Sea Shanty

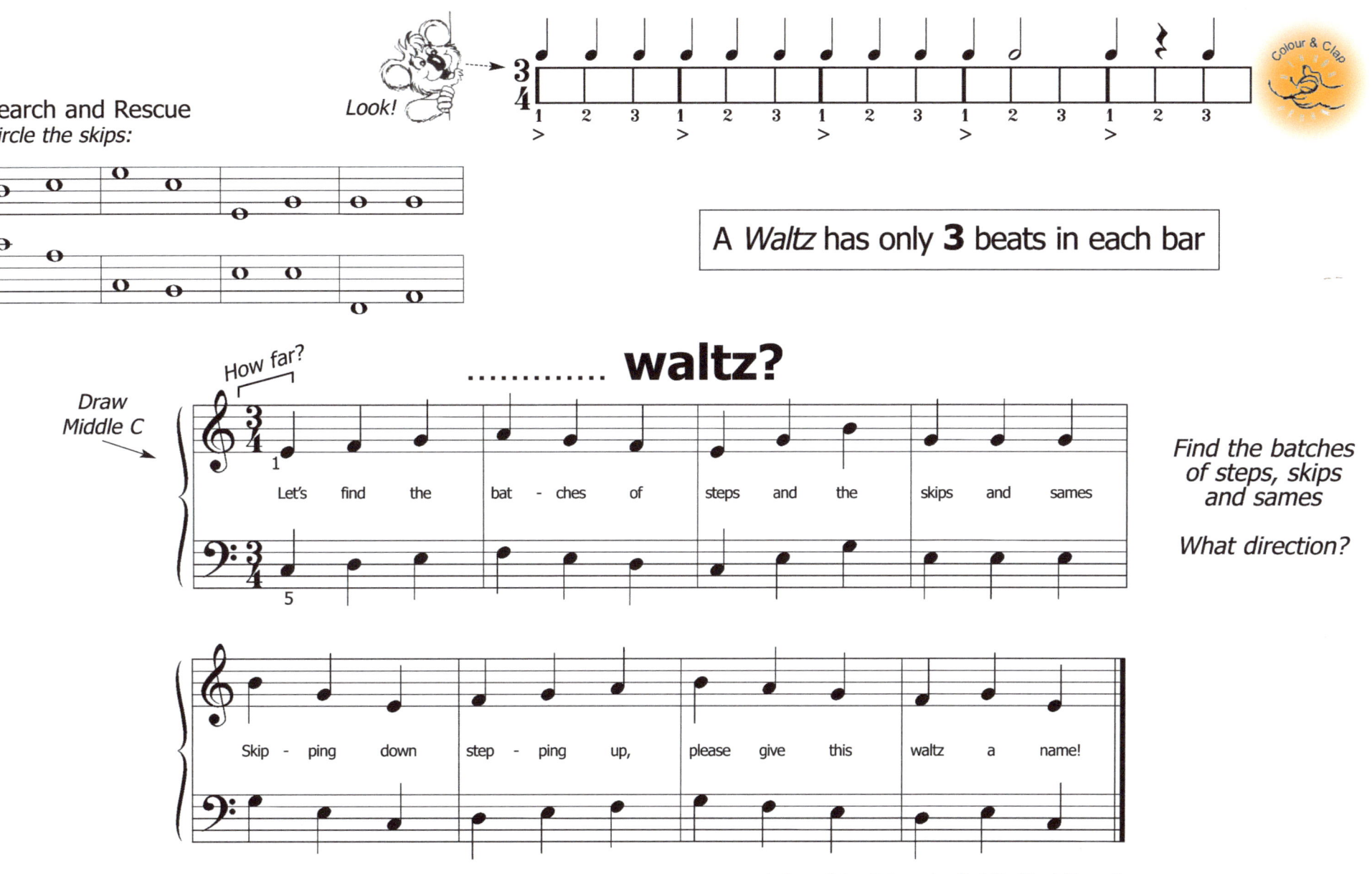

A Spooky Tune

Memory Corner — Name these!

1. 𝄽   2. _(staff)_

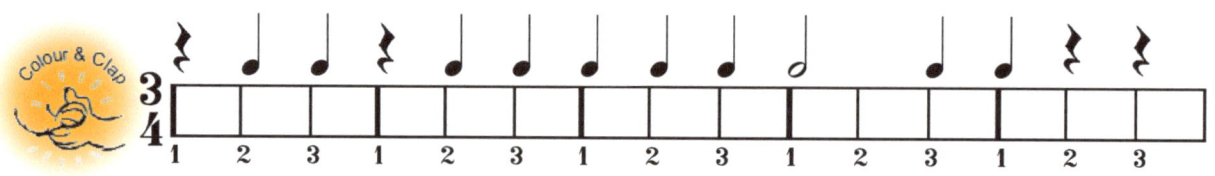
Colour & Clap

Swinging Ghost Song

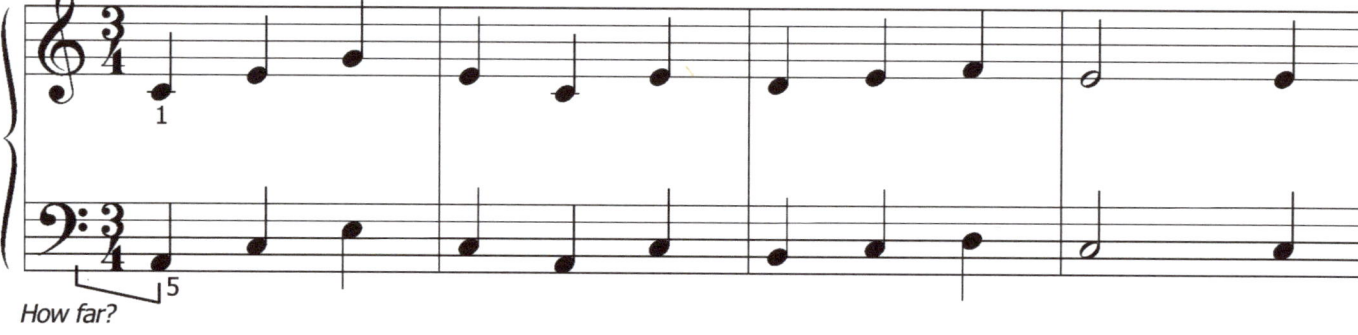

Draw Low C → How far?

Find the batches of skips

Are there batches of steps too?

| Witch - es and | gob - lins and | cast - les and | spells ___ and |
| Ghosts in the | bel - fry who | swing on the | three ___ bells |

★ *Something Extra:* Play 'The Cuckoo' right hand only. See Dexter's Easy Piano Pieces

Playing in March Time

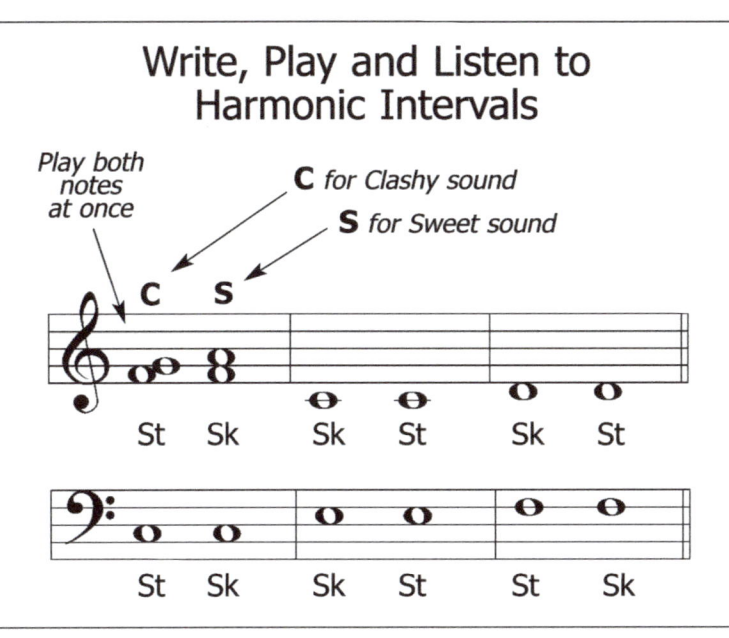

★ Something Extra:
Ask your teacher to show you how to play 'Chop Sticks'
Listen to the Clashy and Sweet sounds

| Elves and | gob - lins | march a - | long_____ |
| While they | march they | sing this | song ||

A Piece To Perform

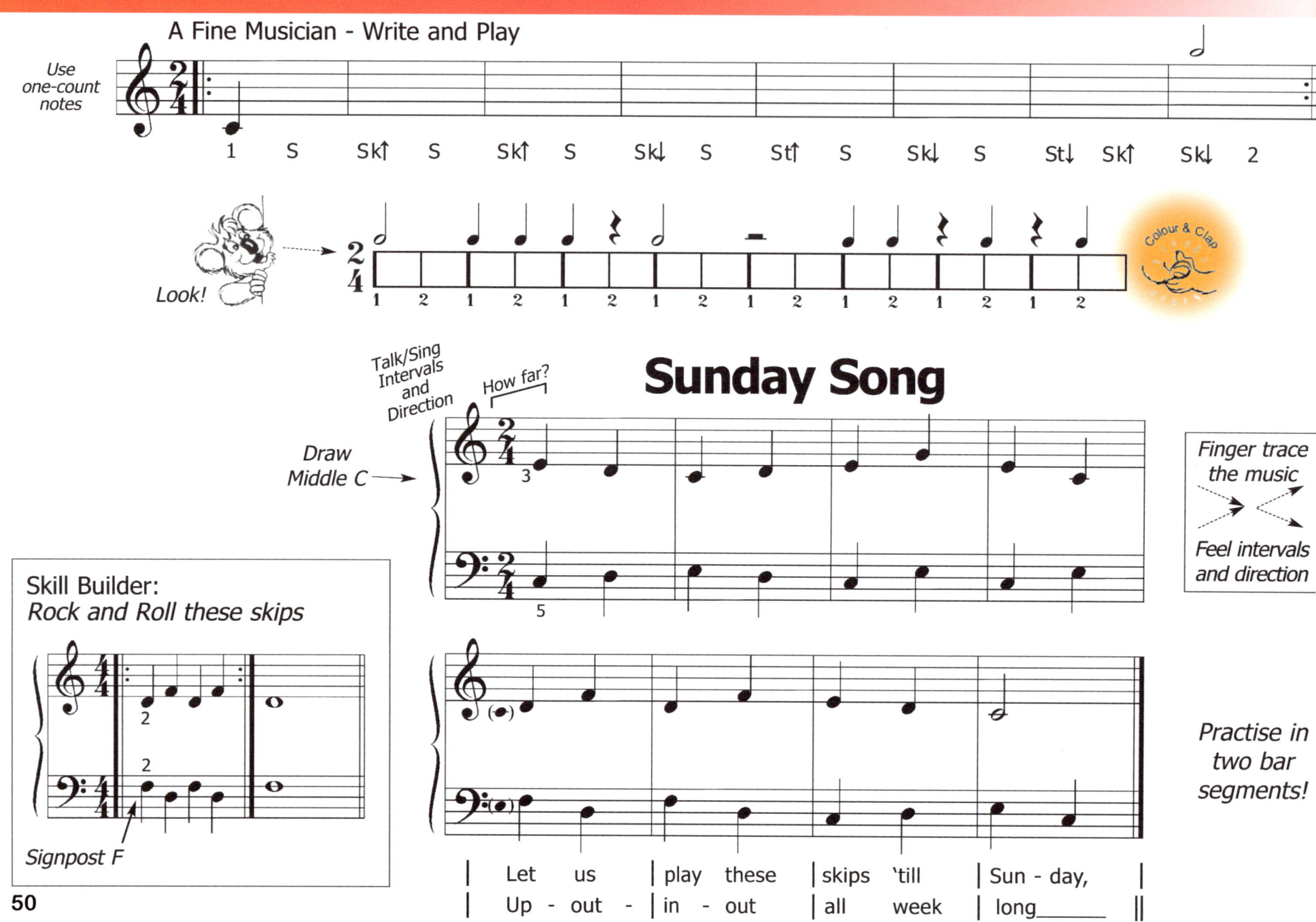

SECTION FOUR - Two New Intervals

The Skip-plus-One (or fourth)
Look, feel, play and listen

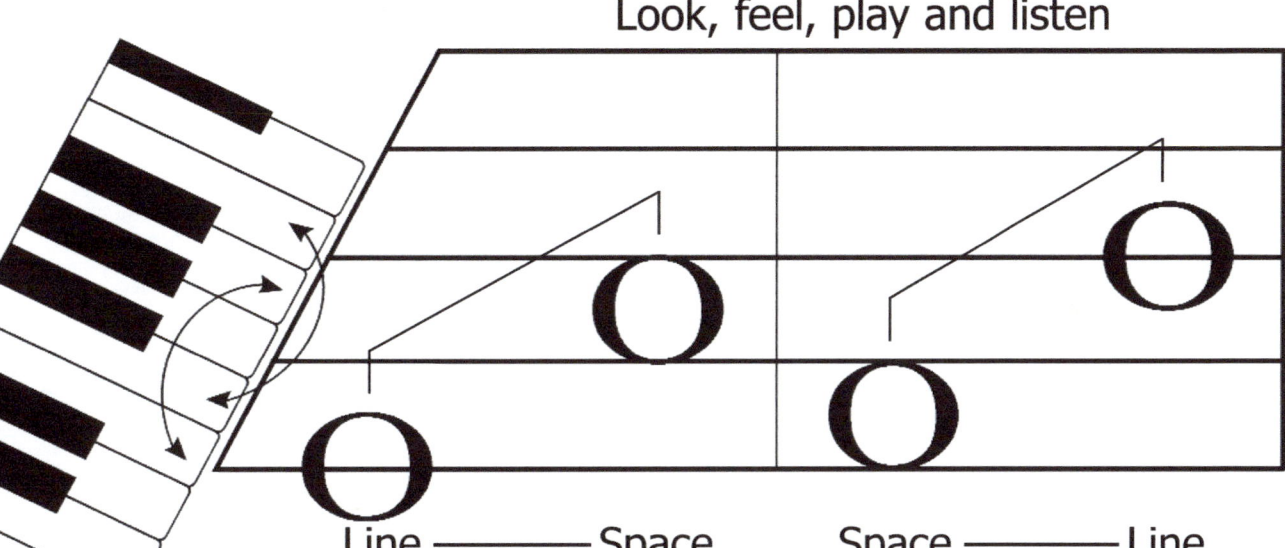

Line ——— Space   Space ——— Line

To play a skip-plus-one feel a skip without sounding it, and go one further
Use either fingers 1 and 4, or 2 and 5

The skip-plus-one is written from a line note to a space note or vice versa.

It is one line or space further than where a skip would be.

Here is how they look on the staff - *Play and Listen*

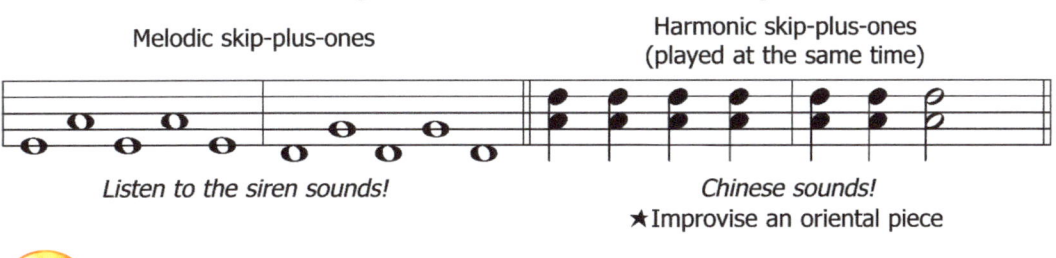

Melodic skip-plus-ones

Harmonic skip-plus-ones
(played at the same time)

Listen to the siren sounds!

Chinese sounds!
★ *Improvise an oriental piece*

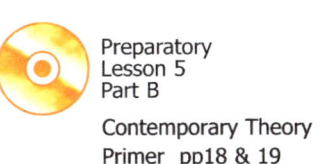

Preparatory
Lesson 5
Part B

Contemporary Theory
Primer pp18 & 19

Write Here!
Skip-plus-ones
Put a dot where the skip would be,
then write your note on the next line or space

Write more skip-plus-ones on manuscript

51

The Jump

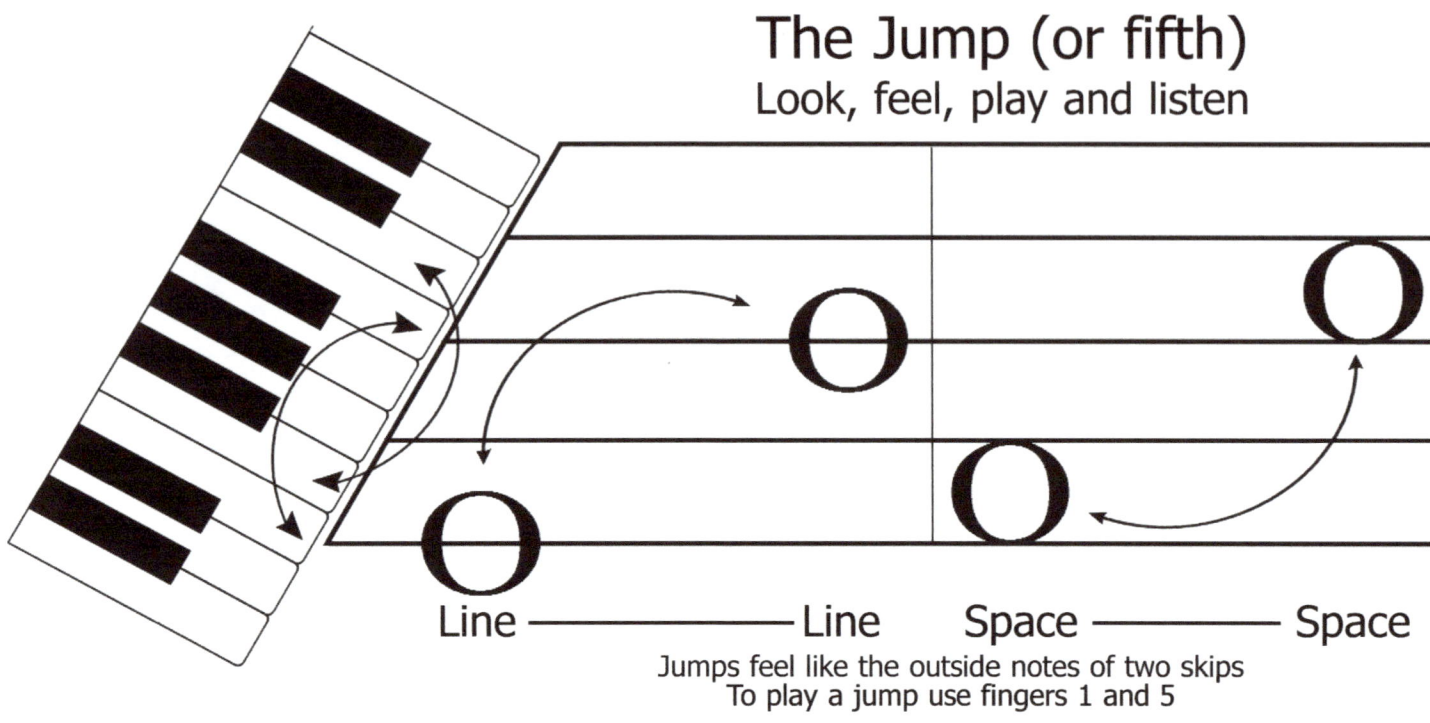

The Jump (or fifth)
Look, feel, play and listen

Line —— Line Space —— Space

Jumps feel like the outside notes of two skips
To play a jump use fingers 1 and 5

The jump looks like the outside notes of two skips together.

The notes jump over a line, or space.

Preparatory Lesson 5 Part B

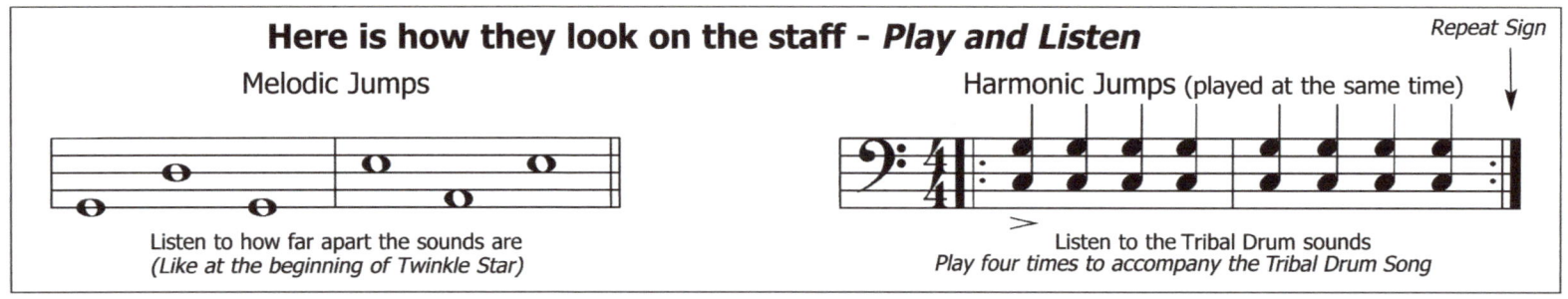

Here is how they look on the staff - *Play and Listen*

Melodic Jumps — Listen to how far apart the sounds are (Like at the beginning of Twinkle Star)

Harmonic Jumps (played at the same time) — Listen to the Tribal Drum sounds. Play four times to accompany the Tribal Drum Song

Repeat Sign

Duet Part

Tribal Drum Song

Composer: Margaret Brandman

A Picture Song To Play

Preparation for playing:
1) *Colour Code* the koalas, by choosing one colour for each type
2) Play the *Interval Drill Game* using plenty of Skip-Plus-Ones and Jumps, with your teacher or parent

Start with the lowest fingers of both hands on two Signpost F's. Remember to find the note by feeling for the three black notes as learnt in your first lesson.

Sound the starting notes: 𝐎 and follow with...

Improvise a song using the intervals of Skip-Plus-One and Jump. Use Harmonic Intervals in the left hand and make up a melody in the right hand. Also try making up a song entirely on the black notes using these intervals. You will find that the sounds are very pleasant.

Refer to:
Contemporary Theory Primer pp20&21

Activity Page

Compare these Intervals

Play and Listen

Write these intervals to match the pictures of Dexter

Write and Play (use two-count notes)

★ *Something Extra: play p14-19 of Contemporary Piano Method 1A*

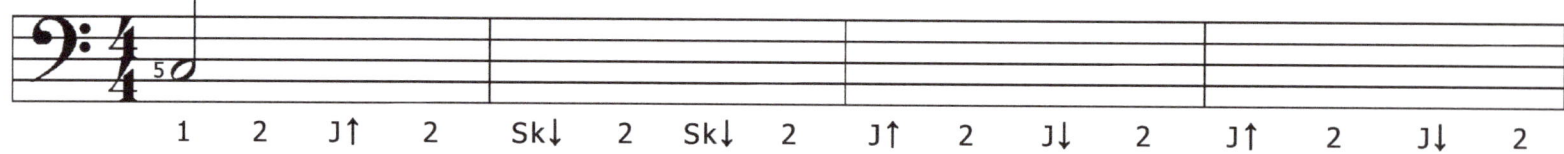

Playing Jumps

Refer to:
Contemporary Theory Primer
pp22 &23

55

Activity Page - Writing

Keyboard Name Games

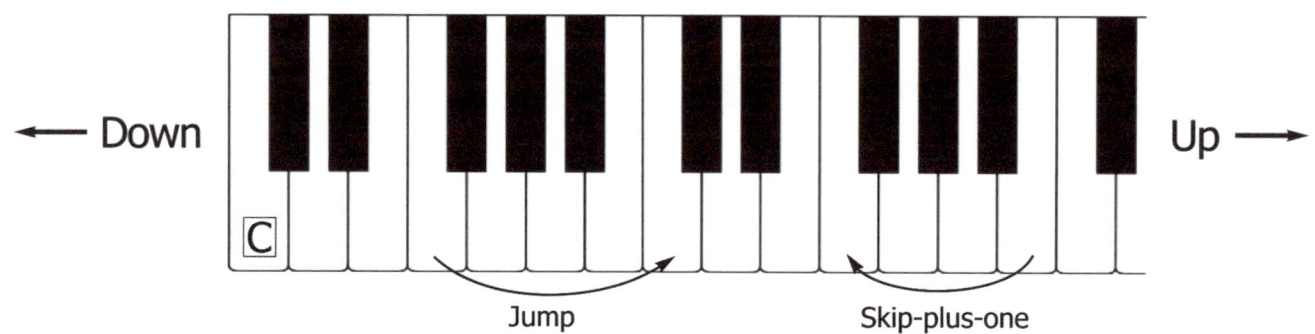

1. Write in the names of the signpost keys, C and F in *Red Pencil*
2. Write in the names of the other keys in ordinary pencil
3. Using arrows to help you work them out, name the keys that are:

   (1) a *Jump* up from C = ...
   (2) a *Skip-plus-one* up from A = ...
   (3) a *Skip* down from D = ...
   (4) a *Step* up from F = ...
   (5) a *Jump* down from E = ...

   (6) a *Skip* up from G = ...
   (7) a *Skip-plus-one* down from F = ...
   (8) a *Step* up from D = ...
   (9) a *Jump* up from F = ...
   (10) a *Skip-plus-one* down from G = ...

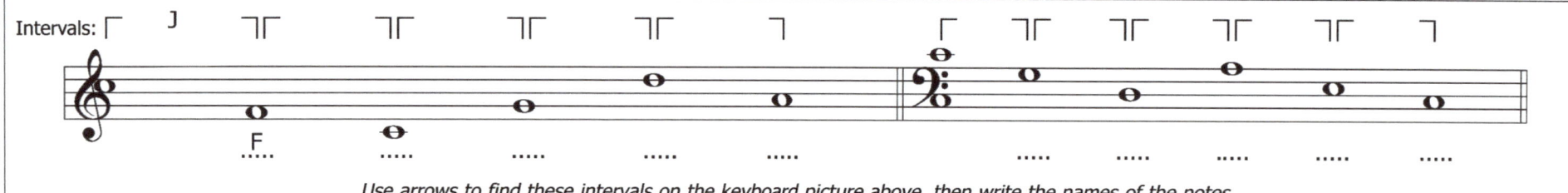

Use arrows to find these intervals on the keyboard picture above, then write the names of the notes

Tunes Using All Five Intervals

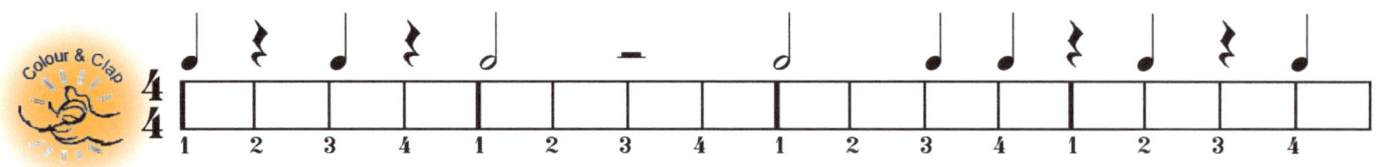

Search and Rescue
Circle the skip-plus-ones

What's The Matterhorn?
(A Swiss Mountain Climbing Song)

Spot the difference!

The *smallest* interval in this song is:

....

The *largest* interval in this song is:

....

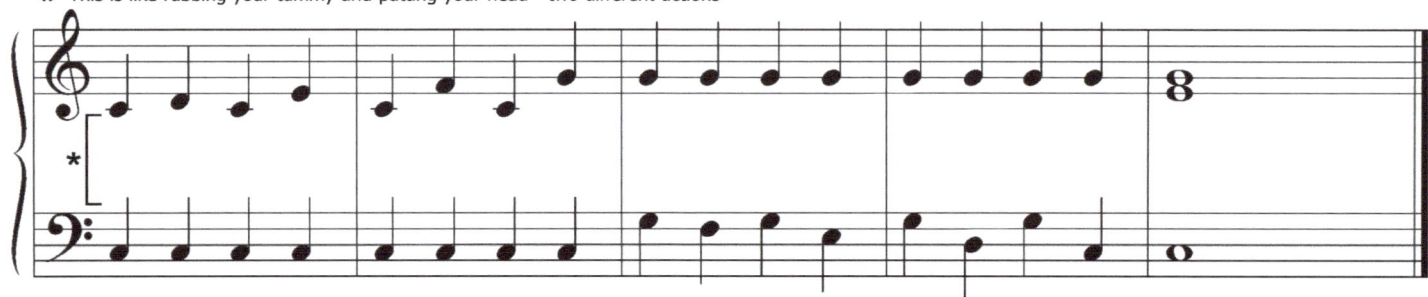

* This is like rubbing your tummy and patting your head - two different actions

| What's the mat - ter | with your horn now? | Is it short or | tall or bright red? |
| Check the size and | spot the diff-erence, | can you see the | Mat-ter-horn a - | head?_____ ||

★ *Something Extra:*
' 'London Bridge' RH only from *Junior Trax*. Complete p24 & 25 of *Contemporary Theory Primer*

58

Quick Quiz — Jumps or Skips?

Colour & Clap

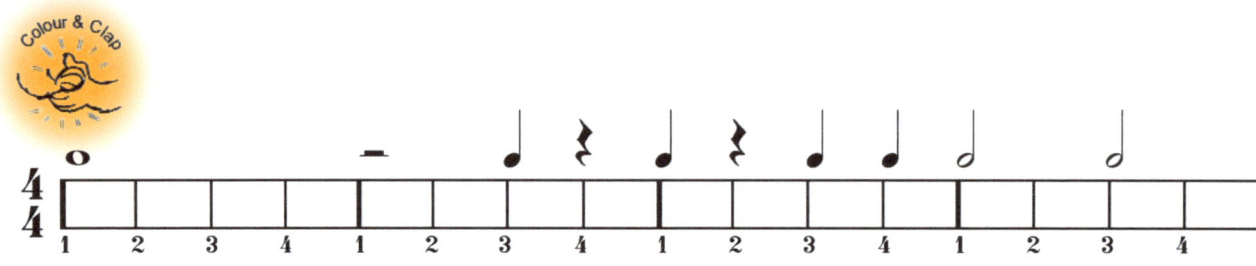

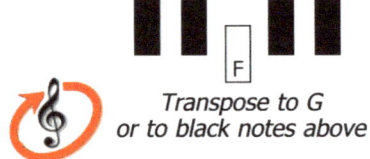

Transpose to G or to black notes above

Johnny Works With One Hammer

Skill Builder

Hold full length

Play four times

| John - ny works with | one ham - mer, | one ham - mer, | one ham - mer, |
| John - ny works with | one ham - mer, | then he works with | two |

Award Certificate

This is to certify that

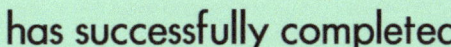

....

has successfully completed

MARGARET BRANDMAN'S
Contemporary Piano Method
Junior Primer

and is promoted to Level 1

....
Date   Teacher

Gude Notes for the Teacher

An expanded version of these guide notes can be found on Margaret Brandman's website:
www.margaretbrandman.com

Key: *CPM 1A* - Contemporary Piano Method Book 1A
 CPM 3 - Contemporary Piano Method Book 3

Parts Of The Piano - page 5: Depending on the age and comprehension of your student, more details as to the workings of the damper mechanism and other parts of the piano could be given to the student. Refer to: CPM 1A - page 6

Finger Numbers - page 7: First demonstrate with both hands fingers 1 through 5 so that students realize the parallels in the fingering system. Next, play a game with your student asking him or her to point the required finger in the air, using either left or right hands. This also helps to reinforce the concepts of right and left.

Lesson Activities - page 12: Spend 5 minutes or so each lesson on improvisation, ear-training actions, gross motor and fine motor drills and/or clapping so as to make each lesson as interesting and engaging as possible.

Gross Motor Actions For Intervals - page 15: If you are able to locate a set of three steps near your studio, ask the child to climb the steps while calling out, or preferably singing the intervals. Say "One", for the starting position and then walk-sing/say "Step Up, Step Up". As you reach the top step sing "Same", as the child puts the other foot down. Then turn around and say "Step Down, Step Down" till you reach the bottom position. Next turn the student around and walk-sing/say "Skip Up", then "Same", (turn on top stair) and then walk-sing/say "Skip Down", to take the student back down. (This is demonstrated on the CPM DVD)

Interval Drill Game - page 15: At this point it is wise to play the Interval Drill Game, as shown on the CPM DVD. Allow the student to place his or her five fingers of either hand over any five consecutive notes (ie: a hand position). You could suggest they begin on one of the signpost notes (C or F). Beginning on the thumb, sound the note, then connect smoothly to notes which are steps up and down, to establish the feeling and the sound of these intervals. Once these are secure, extend the game to include skips and lastly, sames. As students do not have to concern themselves with reading music they will be able to play more involved patterns of intervals than this early stage of reading would allow. This drill therefore will aid the development of finger dexterity and co-ordination as well as solidly impressing on the student the concepts of direction and the intervals. In future lessons, use the Interval Drill Game to develop co-ordination between the hands. Ask the student to play identical intervals in both hands, first in similar motion then in contrary motion. Use the drill game each time a new interval is introduced.

Picture Songs - page 17: The Picture Songs in this book are designed to give students music which uses more intricate finger patterns than they can read at this time. This develops their technique and provides tune material to play until such time as reading skills are at a level to play more complicated tunes. Once the starting note has been sounded, do not repeat it, simply move on to the next intervals.

Rhythm Concepts - Counting and Colouring - page 22: A demonstration of the colour system can be viewed on the CPM DVD. More information on the entire colour system is available on p20 CPM 1A.

The Gestalt Approach - page 25: A unique feature of this method is the simplicity of combining several necessary aspects of music reading and performance into one neat package. By asking the students to say or preferably sing the direction, interval and counting, you are training all vital aspects of music, ear, eye, hand and voice and requiring full concentration on the task at hand. There will be no need for the student to watch their hands on the keyboard. Have the student sing the interval, direction and counting while playing. It is necessary to say "Off", on the first beat after the last bar, as this is the point at which the note must quit (relate this to the colouring on p22).
The learning procedure is as follows:
- Look carefully through the music to see whether the notes move *up or down*.
- Prepare to play by pointing at the notes and saying the intervals, counting and direction.
- One 2 3 4, Step-up 2 3 4, Step-up 2 3 4, Step-down 2 3 4, Step-down 2 3 4 off.
- The students should then talk/sing the information as they play, saying the interval and direction when they see the asterisk (*).

Practice procedure for all pieces written for hands together - page 30:
- Make sure students start on the correct signpost notes with the correct fingers
- After preparing each piece by a talk/sing through, continue to sing the information as you play
- Play separate hands before playing hands together

Gross Motor Actions - page 30: To help the hands co-ordinate, students should use a small tilt of their head to the Right or Left to indicate the directions(up or down). As it is easier for the fingers to move in contrary motion than similar motion in the beginning stages, the head tilt helps the process of combining the movements when playing in similar motion. See the demonstration on the CPM DVD(43.07).

Interval Reading and the keyboard note names - page 32: The Contemporary Piano Method encourages the student to learn the keyboard names of the notes, but does not foster the learning of the note names on the staff, other than the signpost notes. The intention is that when reading music, the most important feature to observe is the interval. By reading in this manner:
- both clefs can be approached in the same way
- fingering for all the notes is not required
- the ear is trained to listen for intervals and
- the students do not need to watch their hands

If the note name is needed for theory purposes, it can always be worked out using a map of the keyboard as on this page.

Practice procedure for tunes in Contrary Motion using two-count notes - page 34: There are several ways your students can talk/sing the music through.
For separate hands:
1) Saying either the interval, direction and the second count : One 2, St up 2, St up 2, St up 2, and so on
2) Saying the interval and the second count only. e.g. One 2, St 2, St 2, St 2, and so on
3) Saying the direction and the second count only. e.g. One 2 , Up 2, Up 2, Up 2, and so on

For hands together:
1)Talk/sing the interval, combined direction and the second count: e.g. One 2, Step-out 2, | Step-out 2, Step out 2 | OR   Step-in 2, Step-in 2 *etc.*
2) Talk/sing only the combined direction and the second count: e.g. One 2, out 2, out 2 *and so on*

For all pieces on the next few pages, make sure your students understand the concepts by using:
- a) Gross Motor Actions - broad actions copying the koala
- b) Fine Motor Actions - touch the page and trace the directions with thumb and forefinger. As shown on the CPM video.

Transposition and Modal Sounds page - 33: (For more information on Modes, refer to CPM 3 and Contemporary Theory Workbook 2 part B) This *Picture Song* can be transposed onto other areas of the keyboard by simply starting with a hand position on any of the other white notes, with the hands one octave apart. This means they may hear some Modal sounds.

Shape and Pattern reading - page 36: Song of Two Hills. Follow the flow by tracing the music with the fingers on the page. There are two ways to talk or sing through this piece.
1) Say both Steps and direction; Step Up, Step Up etc .
2) Direction only: One, up, up, up, | up, down, down, down, | down, up etc (This is useful if the student wishes to play the piece more swiftly)
Once the student can play the intervals correctly they can begin counting four beats in the bar as is usually done.

Finding Hand positions - page 38: From this piece on students should find the hand-positions for themselves, working from the signpost note and the finger number and then placing the fingers accordingly. Sometimes the starting notes are to be judged as a distance from the signpost note. This is so that they become used to beginning on varied starting notes, not just C.

Inserting the second count - page 38: Whenever a two count note appears in tunes which use a mixture of note values, the student needs to remember to say the second count, quite deliberately after saying the interval. To simplify this, the count "2" can be used, no matter whether the music is on the second beat of the bar, or the fourth beat of the bar. See also page 41, for an example of this.

Cuing - page 44: Cuing can be used to help the beginning student become comfortable reading longer pieces of music until such time as the eye movements are swift enough to cope with the larger physical distance between notes at the end of one line and the beginning of the second line. It is helpful for the teacher to copy the final notes of bar four as a cue, in front of the notes in the fifth bar, so that the student can more easily see the interval sizes as they are reading into the fifth bar. This has been demonstrated on this page, but teachers or students can add the cues for themselves if desired from now on.

'Chop Sticks' - pg 48: This is excellent supplementary material at this point, as it emphasizes the sounds of harmonic steps and skips. Teach it by ear, or refer to Hot Trax for the music. Finger the piece using fingers 2, 3, 4 and 5 of each hand, fanning out from F and G starting notes.

Supplementary material - page 55 on:
1. Preparatory Level: Junior Trax pp 5-9 - separate hands only.

2. Contemporary Piano Method 1A: While completing the material in the Junior Primer from page 55 on, students are advised to commence Book 1A of the Contemporary Piano Method, from pp 14 & 15 where separate handed lines of music using mixtures of all the intervals are presented. This helps to consolidate and speed up the reading of all the intervals. If a small amount of reading is set each lesson from pages 14 to 19 in Book 1A, concurrently with the final pages of this book, the student will be ready to play the first piece with varying intervals in the method on page 21 as soon as the Junior Primer is completed.

Varying intervals and timings between the hands - pages 58-60:
These three tunes present the task of playing varying intervals and timings between the hands. 'The Swiss Mountain Climbing Song' presents a group of repeated notes against varying intervals. 'Traffic Lights' and 'Johnny Works With One Hammer', require the student to sustain longer notes in one hand while playing shorter values with the other. Further practice in these skills is presented in the first two songs in Junior Trax.

Follow this book with the material in Junior Trax, together with Contemporary Piano Method 1A for ongoing learning of new skills.

www.ingramcontent.com/pod-product-compliance
Lightning Source LLC
Chambersburg PA
CBHW041952150426

43198CB00004B/108